3

Access Reading

Reading in the Real World

Tim Collins
National-Louis University

Australia Canada Mexico Singapore United Kingdom United States

Access Reading 3: Reading in the Real World
Tim Collins

Publisher: *James W. Brown*
Senior Acquisitions Editor: *Sherrise Roehr*
Director of Product Development: *Anita Raducanu*
Associate Development Editor: *Yeny Kim*
Senior Production Editor: *Lianne Ames*
Director of Marketing, ESL/Global ELT: *Amy Mabley*
Senior Marketing Manager: *Donna Lee Kennedy*
Senior Print Buyer: *Mary Beth Hennebury*
Compositor: *Thompson Steele, Inc.*
Project Manager: *Thompson Steele, Inc.*
Copyeditor: *Thompson Steele, Inc.*
Cover Illustrator: *Nip Rogers*
Cover Designer: *Ha Nguyen*
Text Designer: *Sue Gerould*
Photography Manager: *Sheri Blaney*
Photo Researcher *Jill Engebretson*
Printer: *Edwards Brothers*

Printed in the United States of America.
1 2 3 4 5 6 7 8 9 10 07 06 05 04

For more information contact Heinle, 25 Thomson Place, Boston, Massachusetts 02210 USA, or you can visit our Internet site at http://www.heinle.com

Text Credits: *This Land Is Your Land*, words and music by Woodie Guthrie. TRO—© Copyright 1956 (Renewed) 1958 (Renewed) 1970 (Renewed) Ludlow Music, Inc., New York, NY. Used with Permission.
Take Our Daughters and Sons To Work® is a registered trademark of the Ms. Foundation for Women.

Library of Congress Control Number: 2004104533

ISBN 1-4130-0778-3

Contents

Scope and Sequence iv

To the Teacher viii

Acknowledgments xiv

Photo Credits xiv

To the Learner 1

Unit 1 Getting Along 2

Take a quiz about personality types. Read about teamwork skills at work. Preview a reading before you read. Understand gerunds Use a KWLH chart to help you read.

Unit 2 Around Town 14

Read about a shopping mall. Read a transportation map and schedule. Use maps and drawings to help you read. Review the present tenses. Use maps and drawings.

Unit 3 Keeping Busy 26

Read about wedding customs in the U.S. and around the world. Read a time-off policy from work. Read and make judgments. Understand **used to.** Use calendars.

Unit 4 Money in Your Pocket 38

Read about bank accounts. Read about other services that banks offer. Compare and contrast. Use comparative and superlative adjectives. Use a decision matrix.

Unit 5 Taking Care of Yourself 50

Read about caffeine. Read about getting enough rest. Distinguish between main idea, points, and subpoints. Understand the prefix over-. Use clustering.

Unit 6 Tools and Technology 62

Read about Thomas Edison. Read about the invention of the lightbulb. Decide when to skip unknown vocabulary. Understand the verb **could.** Use a time line.

Unit 7 Our History 74

Read about immigration to the U.S. Read about a multicultural celebration. Check your comprehension while reading. Understand sentences with **before** and **after.** Understand a family tree.

Unit 8 Home Sweet Home 86

Read about smoke detectors. Read about what to do in case of a tornado. Skim for the main idea. Understand simple conditions with **if.** Use a diagram to organize information.

Unit 9 Fun and Relaxation 98

Read about a famous folk song. Read about a famous singer. Distinguish between fact and opinion. Understand linking verbs. Use a scale to show agreement.

Unit 10 Lifelong Learning 110

Read about jobs that are growing in number. Read about teaching children about work. Understand cause-effect relationships. Understand the future tense with **will.** Use a chart to organize information.

Teamwork 122

Learning Journal 126

Vocabulary Index 127

Skills Index 129

Access Reading 3 Scope and Sequence

Unit and Title	Readings	Reading Strategy	Graphic Organizer	Study Skill
1 Getting Along *page 2*	Take a quiz about personality types. Read an advice column about teamwork skills at work.	Preview a reading before you read.	Use a KWLH chart to help you read.	Finding your study style.
2 Around Town *page 14*	Read an article about a shopping mall. Read a bus schedule and a bus route map.	Use maps and drawings to help you read.	Use maps and drawings.	Using an atlas.
3 Keeping Busy *page 26*	Read an article on wedding customs in the U.S. and around the world. Read a time-off policy from work.	Read and make judgments.	Use calendars.	Keeping track of important days.
4 Money in Your Pocket *page 38*	Read a brochure on bank accounts. Read a brochure on bank services.	Compare and contrast.	Use a decision matrix.	Using a decision matrix.
5 Taking Care of Yourself *page 50*	Read an article about caffeine and your health. Read an article on getting enough rest.	Distinguish between main idea, points, and subpoints.	Use clustering.	Staying alert

EFF	SCANS	CASAS
Become and stay informed. Form and express opinions and ideas. Promote family members' growth and development. Work with others. Work within the big picture. Plan and direct growth and development.	Communicate regarding personal information. Understand concepts and materials related to job performance. Demonstrate effectiveness in working with other people. Effectively manage workplace resources. Understand how organizational systems work and work within them.	Allocate time and staff. Work on teams. Work with people of culturally diverse backgrounds. Acquire and evaluate data. Interpret and communicate information. Understand organizational systems. Design systems.
Become and stay informed. Form and express opinions and ideas. Promote family members' growth and development.	Apply principles of budgeting in the management of money. Understand how to locate and use different types of transportation and interpret related travel information. Use leisure time resources and facilities. Understand how social and organizational systems work, and operate effectively within them.	Acquire and evaluate data. Interpret and communicate information. Understand social and organizational systems.
Become and stay informed. Form and express opinions and ideas. Promote family members' growth and development. Strengthen the family system. Work within the big picture.	Communicate regarding personal information. Understand aspects of society and culture. Demonstrate effectiveness in working with other people. Understand concepts and materials related to job performance. Understand how social and organizational systems work, and operate effectively within them.	Allocate time. Work with people of culturally diverse backgrounds. Acquire and evaluate data. Interpret and communicate information. Understand social and organizational systems.
Become and stay informed. Form and express opinions and ideas. Take action to strengthen communities. Meet family needs and responsibilities. Do the work.	Apply principles of comparison-shopping. Use banking services in the community. Use community agencies and services. Communicate effectively in the workplace. Demonstrate effectiveness in working with other people. Understand how social and organizational systems work.	Allocate money. Teach others. Serve customers. Acquire and evaluate data. Interpret and communicate information. Understand social and organizational systems.
Become and stay informed. Form and express opinions and ideas. Promote family members' growth and development. Work within the big picture. Plan and direct growth and development.	Understand basic principles of health maintenance. Understand work-related safety standards and procedures. Understand concepts and materials related to job performance and training.	Allocate time and materials. Acquire and evaluate data. Interpret and communicate information. Understand social and organizational systems. Monitor and correct performance.

Access Reading 3 Scope and Sequence

Unit and Title	Readings	Reading Strategy	Graphic Organizer	Study Skill
6 Tools and Technology *page 62*	Read an article on Thomas Edison's inventions. Read an article on the invention of the lightbulb.	Decide when to skip unknown vocabulary.	Use a time line.	Using a notebook.
7 Our History *page 74*	Read an article on Ellis Island. Read about a multicultural celebration in San Antonio.	Check your comprehension while reading.	Understand a family tree.	Using parts of a textbook.
8 Home Sweet Home *page 86*	Read an article on smoke detectors. Read a public information notice on tornado safety.	Skim for the main idea.	Use a diagram to organize information.	Highlighting important information.
9 Fun and Relaxation *page 98*	Read a biography on Woody Guthrie. Read a biography on Celia Cruz.	Distinguish between fact and opinion.	Use a scale to show agreement.	Relaxing when you study.
10 Lifelong Learning *page 110*	Read an article on good jobs for the future. Read an article on Take Our Daughters and Sons to Work Day.	Understand cause-effect relationships.	Use a chart to organize information.	Using a dictionary.

EFF	SCANS	CASAS
Become and stay informed. Form and express opinions and ideas. Do the work. Work with others.	Understand aspects of society and culture. Demonstrate effectiveness in working with other people. Understand how technological systems work, and operate effectively within them.	Work on teams. Acquire and evaluate data. Interpret and communicate information. Monitor and correct performance. Select equipment and tools. Apply technology to task. Maintain and troubleshoot technology.
Become and stay informed. Form and express opinions and ideas. Work together. Take action to strengthen communities.	Use leisure time resources and facilities. Understand aspects of society and culture. Understand how social systems work, and operate effectively within them.	Work with people from culturally diverse backgrounds. Acquire and evaluate data. Interpret and communicate information. Understand social systems.
Become and stay informed. Form and express opinions and ideas. Work together. Take action to strengthen communities. Promote family members' growth and development. Meet family needs and responsibilities.	Understand concepts of weather. Use community agencies and services. Understand basic health and safety procedures. Understand civic responsibilities. Understand environmental issues. Perform home care skills.	Allocate materials. Teach others. Lead others. Acquire and evaluate data. Interpret and communicate information. Understand technological systems. Monitor and correct performance. Select equipment and tools. Apply technology to task. Maintain and troubleshoot technology.
Become and stay informed. Form and express opinions and ideas. Work together. Take action to strengthen communities. Promote family members' growth and development. Strengthen the family system.	Use leisure time resources and facilities. Understand aspects of society and culture.	Work with people from culturally diverse backgrounds. Acquire and evaluate data. Interpret and communicate information. Understand social systems.
Become and stay informed. Form and express opinions and ideas. Promote family members' growth and development. Meet family needs and responsibilities. Plan and direct personal and professional growth.	Use community agencies and services. Understand aspects of society and culture. Understand basic principles of getting a job. Understand how social and organizational systems work, and operate effectively within them.	Allocate time and money. Acquire and evaluate data. Interpret and communicate information. Understand social and organizational systems.

To the Teacher

Welcome to *Access Reading!*

Access Reading is a standards-based, four-level reading series for adults and young adults. Each level of *Access Reading* consists of:

- a student book
- an instructor's manual
- an audio tape and audio CD
- a Web site: accessreading.heinle.com

Access Reading is based on the Equipped for the Future (EFF) Content Standards, the product of a recent comprehensive six-year study delineating "what adults need to know and be able to do in the 21st century." Thus, the reading topics and skills presented in *Access Reading* center around the three key roles adults play throughout their lives identified in the EFF Standards: family member/parent, community member, and worker.

Access Reading is also compatible with other key skill taxonomies for adult education such as the SCANS Competencies (a U.S. government taxonomy of broad-based skills that workers need to stay competitive in the 21st century) and the CASAS Competencies (a taxonomy of life skills adults need to live independently in the U.S.), as well as various state standards for adult ESL. A complete correlation to the EFF, SCANS, and CASAS Competencies appears in the Scope and Sequence in the front matter of each *Access Reading* student book.

The pedagogy of *Access Reading* is based on current, scientifically based research on reading and on adult learning. Information on the research base of *Access Reading* is in the Instructor's Manual.

The *Access Reading* Student Book

There are 10 thematic units in each student book. Each unit contains two readings. The first reading develops learners' background knowledge and vocabulary, preparing them for the second reading. Each of these readings is based on one of the three adult roles delineated in the EFF Standards. In addition, one of the culminating activities in each unit relates the unit reading and topics to the third adult role in the EFF Standards. For example, in the unit on health, learners first read about caffeine and its effects. In the second reading, they read about being rested for work. In the culminating activities, they relate this knowledge to the community by comparing coffee and tea drinking customs across cultures.

In each unit, learners learn to use a new reading strategy. Throughout each unit, a variety of interactive activities enlivens instruction, and an abundance of exercises checks understanding and ensures that learners are developing target skills and competencies. A unit graphic organizer helps learners develop graphic literacy and reading comprehension skills. A culminating review at the end of each unit allows teachers and learners to determine which skills have been mastered, or whether reteaching or review is necessary to ensure learner success.

Finally, the end matter of each book includes a vocabulary index, a skills index, and a reproducible reading journal.

Teaching a Unit of *Access Reading*

Each unit of *Access Reading* is designed to take four to five class hours to teach. However, it can be expanded through more paired and small group activities, more time for discussion, and more time spent on the activities and exercises.

Use these suggestions as you teach each page of *Access Reading.*

- Have learners talk about the pictures or illustrations on the page.
- Help learners read the directions for each activity.
- Model activities for learners as necessary.
- Allow time for learners to follow the directions and complete each activity.
- Check learner results before going on to the next exercise or activity, providing additional reinforcement as necessary.

Accessing Information

Each unit of *Access Reading* begins with a four-page Accessing Information section.

The one-page unit opener uses pictures and discussion prompts to build interest in and purposes for reading.

- Use the illustrations to develop learners' background knowledge. Have learners identify the people, places, and objects; say what the people are doing; and imagine what the people are saying.

- Use the questions in Talk About It and You Decide to build purposes for learning. Have learners talk over their answers in pairs or small groups and then share their answers with the class.
- Use the skills box to present the unit's goals to learners and to guide your lesson planning throughout the unit.

The second page of Accessing Information begins with a Key Vocabulary section and is followed by a reading strategy preview, Before You Read. The Key Vocabulary section develops key vocabulary related to the entire unit. Before You Read is a short exercise that allows learners to try the unit's target reading strategy before it is formally presented later in the unit.

- Have learners use background knowledge to brainstorm known vocabulary about the unit topic.
- Have learners use the pictures and illustrations on the page to learn the new vocabulary. Then have learners complete the reinforcement exercise.

The third page of Accessing Information contains the first reading, and an accompanying piece of realia.

- Have learners read the selection and the realia independently.
- Next, play the audio tape/CD as learners follow along silently.
- Before going on to the comprehension exercises on the next page, check comprehension by asking a few simple questions.

On the fourth page of Accessing Information, post-reading exercises check comprehension, develop the unit reading strategy, and allow learners to integrate understanding of the material they just read. In the interactive Teamwork activity, learners engage in cooperative learning.

Giving Voice

After Accessing Information, a one-page Giving Voice section allows learners to relate the reading topic to their own needs and realities, so that they begin to use their new knowledge to effect meaningful changes in their lives.

Accessing Information

Next, a second five-page Accessing Information section builds toward the unit's second reading. The first page reprises the first reading's content and vocabulary through discussion and a new piece of realia. Use this page to activate learners' prior learning and to orient newcomers or absentees.

- Use peer teaching to ensure that newcomers and absentees have the requisite vocabulary and background knowledge to successfully tackle the reading on the next page.

The second page formally presents the unit's target reading strategy.

- Have learners read the unit reading strategy. Clarify as necessary.

The next two pages contain the second reading.

- Have learners read the selection independently.
- Next, play the audio tape/CD as learners follow along silently.
- Before going on to the comprehension exercises that follow the reading, check comprehension by asking a few simple questions.

Following the second reading, post-reading exercises check comprehension, develop the unit reading strategy, and allow learners to integrate understanding of the material they read.

Taking Action, Bridging to the Future, and Connection

The Taking Action, Bridging to the Future, and Connection sections bring each unit of *Access Reading* to culmination. In these sections, learners relate the reading topics to the third EFF role not yet covered in the readings and learn skills to apply their new knowledge to their lives.

Enriching Your Vocabulary and Language Note

At key teachable moments throughout *Access Reading*, learners are introduced to level-appropriate vocabulary (Enriching Your Vocabulary) and grammar (Language Note) pulled directly from the readings in order to help them read more effectively.

Study Skill

Also at a key teachable moment in each unit, a Study Skill is presented to help learners improve their learning skills. These study skills are directly related to the content of the unit. For example, in the unit on technology, learners read about Thomas Edison's notebooks. Then they read about ways they can use their notebooks.

- Have learners read the information. Clarify as necessary.
- Ask learners to give examples of how they, or other members of their families, might use the suggestion to learn more effectively.

Review

Finally, a one-page Review checks learner understanding of the reading strategy and other skills developed in the unit. Teachers may use this page for review or to ensure learners are ready for the reproducible test in the Instructor's Manual.

- Have learners look over the page for a few minutes. Model the directions if necessary.
- When learners are ready, have them complete the activities. Then check learners' work. Reteach or review as necessary before having the learners complete the reproducible test in the Instructor's Manual.

 Your Portfolio

A portfolio assessment activity on the Review page allows teachers to build a portfolio assessment system. A portfolio assessment system allows learners to gather samples of their best work and keep them in a file folder or box. As learners add materials to their portfolios, they will be able to observe growth in their skills and have tangible evidence to document their learning.

- Review each learner's or group's work. Ask learners to say what they learned from the activity, in which areas they want to develop improved skills, and which of their skills have improved over the course of the unit.
- When learners are ready, have them place their completed work in their portfolios.

For more information on setting up a portfolio assessment system, see the *Access Reading* Instructor's Manual.

Summing Up

At the end of each unit, a second skills section reprises the skills presented in the skills box on the unit opener, this time with check-off boxes. Checking off the boxes will provide learners with a sense of pride and accomplishment.

- Help the learners read the skills. Clarify vocabulary as needed.
- Have learners check the boxes that apply to them. Help each learner write a new skill of his or her own on the line and check that box. Check their work. Reteach or review as necessary until all learners can check all the boxes.

Access Reading Instructor's Manual

The *Access Reading* Instructor's Manual contains a complete answer key for exercises in the student book and a complete assessment system. Included in the assessment system are:

- Instructions for setting up a portfolio assessment system.
- Multiple-choice analysis questions to help prepare students for standardized testing.
- Suggestions for ongoing informal assessment throughout each unit.
- Reproducible tests for each unit that give programs and teachers the option of assessing learners formally at regular intervals.

The Instructor's Manual also includes:

- Suggestions for presenting new key vocabulary and structures.
- Complete suggestions for presenting each reading.
- Teaching notes for key exercises and activities.
- Suggestions for previewing and presenting the unit reading strategy.
- Ideas for enriching and enlivening instruction.

Access Reading Web Site

The *Access Reading* Web site contains additional readings and activities. The Web site readings extend the themes presented in the unit readings. The Web site activities can be used as a review and a reinforcement of the skills and vocabulary taught in the student book. The *Access Reading* Web site address is **accessreading.heinle.com.**

Acknowledgments

Many, many people have contributed to *Access Reading*. First, I would like to acknowledge the individuals at Heinle who made this book possible. I'd like to thank Jim Brown, Sherrise Roehr, and Ingrid Wisniewska for listening to the initial concept, believing in it, and providing constant feedback and support as we developed and tested prototypes and sample units and as the manuscript for each book took shape. I'd also like to acknowledge my gratitude to Yeny Kim for her super editing, constant support, and encouragement during the development of the manuscript. Anita Raducanu's careful management of each stage made the whole editorial process go smoothly. Credit for the design and production go to Lianne Ames of the Heinle production department and Nancy Freihofer and her staff of collaborators at Thompson Steele. Their careful work helped convert the manuscript into the attractive, well laid-out book you hold in your hands today. I'd also like to thank Donna Lee Kennedy of Heinle's marketing department for her help and encouragement throughout the development of this series.

I am also very grateful to the adult educators from around the country who reviewed various stages of the manuscript—invaluable feedback that helped make this book appropriate for classrooms nationwide.

Mona S. Brantley, *Des Moines Area Community College, Ankeny, IA;* Rocio Castiblanco, *Seminole Community College, Sanford, FL;* Marlon Davis, *Education Service Center, San Antonio, TX;* Tim Doyle, *San Mateo Adult School, San Mateo, CA;* Renee B. Klosz, *Lindsey Hopkins Technical Educational Center, Miami, FL;* Ronna Magy, *Los Angeles Unified School District, Los Angeles, CA;* David Red, *Fairfax Adult Education, Fairfax, VA;* Anne W. Savidge, *Richland College, Dallas, TX*

At National-Louis University, I'd like to thank Leah Miller, Darrell Bloom, Bernadette Herman, Diane Salmon, Alison Hilsabeck, and Elizabeth Hawthorne for not only encouraging me to write, but also for helping me carve out the time from my other responsibilities to write this series.

I'd also like to express my appreciation to Mary Jane Maples, who taught me so many of the skills I used in writing this book. I also owe a debt of gratitude to Bob Wilson for his advice and guidance over the years.

Finally, I'd like to thank my parents for giving me the gift of reading. I hope that through this book adult learners gain the reading skills that they need to reach their hopes, goals, and dreams.

Photo Credits

All photographs not otherwise credited are owned by © Heinle, a part of the Thomson Corporation.

xv top right: © Walter Hodges/CORBIS; xv center right: © Ed Eckstein/CORBIS; xv bottom right: © PhotoDisc/Getty Images

Unit 1
2 left: © Kindra Clineff/Index Stock Imagery; 2 top right: © IT STOCK INT'L/Index Stock Imagery; 7 top: © KARL MATHIS/EPA/ Landov; 7 bottom: © Hulton Archive/Getty Images

Unit 2
14 left: © Christina Kennedy/Photo Edit; 14 top right: © PhotoDisc Green/Getty Images; 14 bottom right: © Robert Holmes/CORBIS; 16 top: © AP Photo/Jim Mone, File; 16 bottom: © BILL ALKOFER/Bloomberg News/Landov

Unit 3
26 left: © Kaluzny-Thatcher/Stone/Getty Images; 26 top right: © Eric K. K. Yu/CORBIS; 26 bottom right: © Stuart McClymont/ Stone/Getty Images; 28 bottom left: © Nik Wheeler/CORBIS; 28 bottom center: © Robert Holmes/CORBIS

Unit 4
38 left: © Kent Dufault/Index Stock Imagery; 38 top right: © David Young-Wolff/Photo Edit; 38 bottom right: © Michael Newman/Photo Edit

Unit 5
50 left: © Jim McGuire/Index Stock Imagery; 50 top right: © Royalty-Free/CORBIS; 50 bottom right: © Paul Barton/CORBIS; 55: © PhotoDisc Green/Getty Images

Unit 6
62 left: © North Wind Picture Archives; 62 top right: © Bettmann/ CORBIS; 62 bottom right: © LWA-Dann Tardif/CORBIS; 64: © Hulton Archive/Getty Images; 67: © Jeff Greenberg/The Image Works

Unit 7
74 left: © Bob Daemmrich/The Image Works; 74 top right: © Bettmann/CORBIS; 74 bottom right: © Sandy Felsenthal/ CORBIS; 76: © Henryk T. Kaiser/Index Stock Imagery; 79: © Philip Gould/CORBIS; 81: © Alan Carey/The Image Works; 85: © PhotoDisc Red/Getty Images

Unit 8
86 left: © ANDREAS MANOLIS/Reuters/Landov; 86 top right: © Tony Freeman/Photo Edit; 86 bottom right: © Jeff Greenberg/ Photo Edit; 93 top right: © JOHN SOMMERS/Reuters/Landov; 93 bottom right: © PhotoDisc/Getty Images

Unit 9
98 left: © Kevin Winter/Getty Images; 98 top right: © CBS/ Landov; 98 bottom right: © BSIP Agency/Index Stock Imagery; 100: © John Springer Collection/CORBIS 103: Courtesy of the Union Pacific Historical Collection; 105: © AFP PHOTO/Lucy Nicholson/CORBIS

Unit 10
110 left: © Robert E. Daemmrich/Stone/Getty Images; 110 top right: Photo courtesy of the Ms. Foundation for Women; 110 bottom right: © BSIP Agency/Index Stock Imagery; 115: © Rick Leckrone/Index Stock Imagery; 117: © Ronnie Kaufman/CORBIS; 118: © Ariel Skelley/CORBIS

To the Learner

Your Job

Welcome to *Access Reading!*

This book will help you learn to read better. In this book, you will read about all parts of your life—in your job, your community, and your family.

You will learn many things in this book. You will learn to read more quickly. You will learn vocabulary. You will learn grammar. You will learn study skills. You will learn speaking skills.

What do you want to learn from this book? Check the box or boxes. Then follow the instructions.

What do you want to learn? I want to	Instructions
☐ 1. Improve my vocabulary.	Pay attention to the Key Vocabulary and Enriching Your Vocabulary sections.
☐ 2. Improve my reading skills.	Pay attention to the Reading Strategy sections.
☐ 3. Improve my grammar.	Pay attention to the Language Note sections.
☐ 4. Improve my study skills.	Pay attention to the Study Skill sections.
☐ 5. Use new information to improve my life.	Pay attention to the Giving Voice, Taking Action, Connection and Bridging to the Future sections.
☐ 6. Improve my speaking skills.	Pay attention to the Talk About It, Talk It Over, Teamwork, and You Decide sections.
☐ 7. Check my learning.	Pay attention to the Review page and the Portfolio activity.

Your Community

Your Family

Getting Along

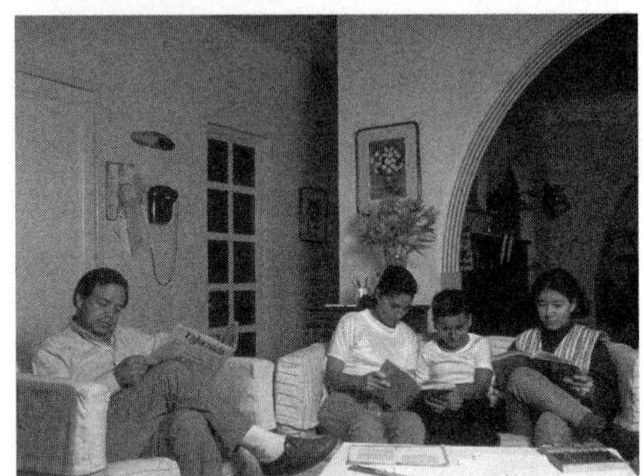

In this unit, you will:

1. Take a quiz about personality types.
2. Read about teamwork skills at work.
3. Preview a reading before you read.
4. Understand gerunds.
5. Use a KWLH chart to help you read.

Accessing Information

Talk About It

Look at the pictures. What are the people doing? Are they getting along? Which ones probably like being alone? Which ones like being around lots of other people?

You Decide

Do you like to be alone or with just a few close friends? Or do you enjoy being around a lot of different people? Why?

Key Vocabulary

A. In this unit, you will read about different personality types. You will also read about teamwork skills at work. First, work with a partner. What words can you use to describe people's personalities? In your notebook, write a list of words.

B. Study the vocabulary.

introvert–quiet person who likes to be alone or with only a few people

extrovert–person who likes to be with many people

outgoing–likes talking to people and meeting new people

cooperate–work together

communicate–give information to other people

compromise–agreement in which each person gives up something in order to agree

role–person's job or task in a group

teamwork–working with a group of people

EXERCISE 1 Vocabulary

Write the word from Key Vocabulary, part B on the line.

1. Repairing this truck is a big job. The mechanics need to use ________________ to get the job done on time.
2. An ________________ likes going to parties.
3. An ________________ likes working on projects alone.
4. Mary has lots of friends. She is always busy talking to them on the phone, sending them e-mail, and going out with them. Mary is really ________________.
5. In our team, Patty and Selwa answer the phones and talk to customers. Abdul takes care of the paperwork. And Mrs. Osnaya is the manager. Each person has a different ________________.

EXERCISE 2 Before You Read

Look over the reading on page 4. Read the title, look at the pictures, read the captions, read the first paragraph, and look at the box after the reading. What is the main idea? Write a few words on the line.

____

What's a "People Person"?

CD 1 TRACK 1

ARE YOU A "PEOPLE PERSON"?

Extrovert

A "people person" is someone who enjoys being with people. Another name for a "people person" is an extrovert. Extroverts are outgoing. They enjoy going to parties, talking to people, and making new friends. Introverts are the opposite. They like being alone or with small groups of friends or family members. They're often shy. Which one are you? Take the quiz and find out.

1. A fun Saturday night for you is:
   a. Watching TV at home.
   b. Going to a party.
   c. Working on a project at home.
   d. Going out to eat with a group of friends.
2. You are on a long airplane trip. What do you do?
   a. Read quietly.
   b. Get to know the person sitting next to you.
   c. Sleep.
   d. Call a friend on your cell phone before you get on the plane.
3. You just got a big raise and promotion at work. What do you do?
   a. Buy yourself a nice present.
   b. Call all your friends and relatives right away.
   c. Not tell anyone because you feel embarrassed.
   d. Tell your best friend at work.
4. Are you ever lonely?
   a. No, I like to be by myself.
   b. No, I am always with other people.
   c. Yes, but it doesn't bother me.
   d. Yes, but I'm usually with my friends.
5. You have a new neighbor. What do you do?
   a. Nothing.
   b. Get to know the new neighbor right away.
   c. Smile and say hello, but avoid talking.
   d. Help the neighbor move in and get settled.
6. You are shopping and have a question about a product. What do you do?
   a. Read the label to find the answer.
   b. Ask an employee for help.
   c. Put the product back on the shelf. Then ask a friend the question later.
   d. Ask another customer.

Introvert

Answers

For each **b** or **d** answer, give yourself 1 point. Add up your points, and then check your score.

Scores

0 to 2: **Introvert.** You probably enjoy staying at home. You might enjoy quiet activities such as reading or listening to music. You may have only a few friends, but you are probably close to them. Going to a party or meeting new people can be hard for you. You may, however, enjoy being with relatives or friends.

3 to 4: **Mixture of Introvert and Extrovert.** Sometimes you want to be alone, and other times you enjoy being with others. You may not have a lot of friends, but you are close to them.

5 to 6: **Extrovert.** You are friendly and outgoing, and you enjoy spending time with people. However, you may have trouble doing things alone, such as studying for a test. Even extroverts need time alone, so take time each day to focus on yourself.

EXERCISE 3 After You Read

A. Review your answer to Exercise 2 on page 3. Was your answer correct? Do you want to change your answer? Write a few words on the line.

____

B. Write the answers in your notebook.

1. What is an introvert? An extrovert?
2. What kinds of activities do introverts like?
3. What kinds of activities do extroverts like?

EXERCISE 4 Introvert or Extrovert?

Are the people introverts or extroverts? Write **introvert** or **extrovert** on the line.

____________ **1.** Every night, Miguel goes to his garage and works on his car. He enjoys fixing it and making it run better. On weekends, he goes for long drives alone in the country.

____________ **2.** After work, Wu-sen calls her friends to talk about her day. Sometimes she's on the phone for three or four hours.

____________ **3.** Lisa loves going to the library to study. She likes to sit at a quiet table behind the bookshelves.

____________ **4.** Samuel communicates with his friends using e-mail several times a day. He has e-mail friends in many places around the world.

Teamwork

A. Work with a small group. How many people in your group are introverts? Extroverts? A mixture? Use your results from the quiz on page 4 to make a bar graph. Use the graph paper on page 122. Follow the example.

B. Work with your class. Use your group bar graphs to make a class bar graph. Then talk over the results. Are there a lot of introverts in your class? Extroverts?

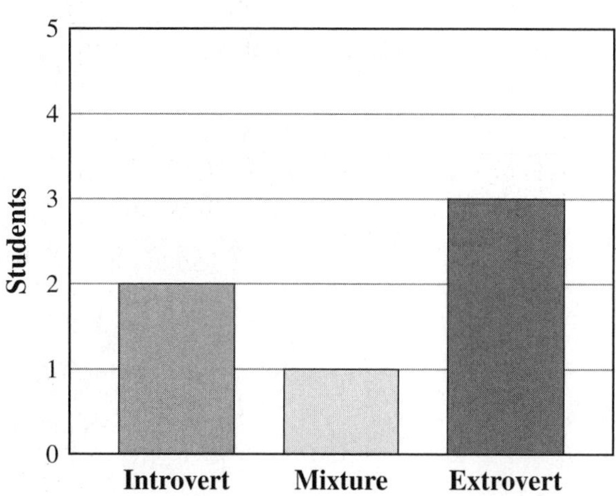

Giving Voice

Talk It Over

Work with a partner. Think about your result on the quiz. Do you agree? Are you really an introvert or an extrovert? Why? Share your partner's answer with the class.

EXERCISE 5 Help for Introverts and Extroverts

A. There is nothing wrong with being an introvert or an extrovert. But sometimes, introverts need to talk more. Sometimes extroverts need to be quiet and pay attention to others, too. Look at the sentences. How can introverts overcome their shyness? How can extroverts take the time to listen to others? Write the number in the box.

Ways introverts can overcome their shyness	
Ways extroverts can pay attention to others	

1. If you find that you are talking a lot, stop talking and ask a question. Then wait for others to answer.
2. If you feel afraid to talk to people at a party, find another person who is alone. Talk to that person.
3. When talking with several people, allow each person to have a turn speaking before speaking again.
4. Write down what you are going to say before you have to say it.

B. Work with a partner. Write two lists in your notebook. Write more ways introverts can overcome shyness and extroverts can pay attention to others. Share your lists with the class.

LANGUAGE NOTE
Gerunds

A gerund is a verb that we use as a noun. A gerund ends in **-ing.**

Watching TV is fun.

I like **watching** TV.

Review the reading on page 4. Circle the gerunds.

Accessing Information

Famous But Shy

Introverts aren't quiet all the time. Read about these famous shy people.

Gloria Estefan

The famous singer Gloria Estefan was very shy when she was young. She liked to sing and play the guitar in her bedroom. She didn't like to talk to people or sing for them. But her teachers encouraged her to join a band. In the band she met her future husband, Emilio Estefan. He helped her use her singing to become famous.

Abraham Lincoln

This great president was very shy. Lincoln was from a poor family, and he grew up in the country. He couldn't go to school for very long, so he taught himself. He didn't feel comfortable talking to people because he was from the country and had little education. His friend, Joshua Speed, helped him. Speed invited him to parties and introduced him to people. Little by little, Lincoln felt more comfortable with people. Because of Speed, Lincoln was able to run for Congress and to ask his future wife to marry him.

Talk About It

Is it surprising that Lincoln and Estefan were shy? Why? Do people usually think of leaders and entertainers as shy? Why? Were Lincoln and Estefan really introverts all their lives? Or did they change from introverts to extroverts over time? Why do you think so?

You Decide

Is it easy to get along with an introvert? An extrovert? Why do you think so? What makes a person easy to get along with? Why?

STUDY SKILL
Finding Your Study Style

Introverts and extroverts study differently. Are you an extrovert? You might want to do homework with a friend or a group of people. Are you an introvert? You probably like to study alone in a quiet room. Think about your personality, and find ways to study that are best for you.

READING STRATEGY
Preview a Reading Before You Read

It's easier to read when you preview a reading first. When you preview a reading, you should:

1. Read the title and the headings.
2. Look at the pictures and the captions.
3. Read the first sentence of each paragraph.

EXERCISE 6 Previewing a Reading

Follow the three steps for previewing a reading with the reading on pages 9 and 10. What is the reading about? Write a few words on the line.

____

EXERCISE 7 Before You Read

Before you read, you should try to figure out the main idea. Then ask two questions:

1. What do I know about the topic?
2. What do I want to learn about the topic?

After you read, you should ask:

3. What did I learn?
4. How will I learn more about the topic?

A KWLH chart can help you answer these questions. K means "know," W means "want," L means "learned," and H means "how." Look at the KWLH chart.

Main idea of the reading: ______________________________

K What I know about the topic	W What I want to know about this topic	L What I learned about this topic	H How I will learn more about this topic

Look at the main idea you wrote in Exercise 6. Write it on the line above the KWLH chart. Complete the K and W columns. Then read the article on pages 9 and 10.

CD 1 TRACK 2

At Work

by Carla Carson

Teamwork is important

DEAR CARLA,

I am a medical assistant at a large clinic, and I work for a very nice doctor named Dr. Lee. I check all of Dr. Lee's patients before she sees them. I also fill out forms and paperwork for Dr. Lee and help her nurse. However, my job is changing. I will work with three doctors, three nurses, and two more medical assistants. I am really worried. What if we don't get along?

Signed,
Daisy Wilson

DEAR DAISY,

Your situation is not unusual. More and more workplaces are using teams to get the job done. Companies think teams are good because people with different skills can cooperate to get the work done together. Because each person has different skills, the group is stronger than any of the individuals.

In order for teamwork to be successful, a number of things have to happen:

1. Employees have to cooperate. When you work alone, you just focus on your work. When you are on a team, the team has to work together. One day you may be very busy. Then your coworkers can help you. Another day, a coworker may be very busy. Then you can help him or her.

2. Employees have to communicate. When you work alone, you don't have to communicate very much with many workers. However, soon you will have eight coworkers. Communication will become a big part of your job. You will have to communicate clearly. You will also have to listen carefully to make sure you understand.

3. Employees need clear roles. For example, you know that someone has to go to the lab every day to pick up patients' test results. The lab is far from your office. So you walk there. On your way, you meet a coworker who is coming from the lab. You both went to the lab because your roles weren't clear. Clear roles also help the team do all the work. For example, you think that a coworker is getting the results from the lab, but she thinks that you will get them. So no one gets the lab results, and the doctors are angry! On good teams, workers know their roles and do them every day.

With cooperation, communication, and clear roles, you will have a great team!

continued 

DEAR CARLA,

I work for a cleaning company. Late at night we clean company offices. But I have a problem with one of the employees. Her name is Marcia. She is friendly and a hard worker, but she has a bad habit. When she cleans the bathrooms, she sings! She's a terrible singer. We can hear her everywhere in the building. We have asked her to stop, but she says that she likes to sing while she cleans the bathrooms. We like Marcia, but we can't stand her singing! What can we do?

Signed,
Tired of Singing

DEAR TIRED OF SINGING,

You have a common problem. Many times, our coworkers' habits bother us. But your problem seems worse than usual. Maybe you can compromise. A compromise is a solution that is good for everyone. Each person has to give up something, but each person also gets something. So here are two ideas:

1. You say that Marcia sings when she cleans the bathrooms. If other employees clean the bathrooms, then Marcia won't sing. Maybe you will have to clean the bathrooms, but you won't hear Marcia singing.

2. If Marcia won't stop cleaning the bathrooms, get a radio with earphones. When Marcia sings, turn on the radio. Then you won't hear her.

EXERCISE 8 Completing the KWLH Chart

A. Review your answers to Exercise 7 on page 8. Did filling out the first two columns of the KWLH chart help you read? Why? Tell your partner. Share your partner's answer with the class.

B. Think about the reading. What did you learn about teamwork at work? How will you learn more? Complete the L and H columns of the KWLH chart. Share your answers with the class.

EXERCISE 9 Answer the Questions

Write the answers in your notebook.

1. Who does Daisy work with now?
2. Who will be on Daisy's new team?
3. Why is she worried?
4. Are a lot of companies using teams these days?
5. Why do companies like teams?
6. What should employees on teams do?
7. Why is cooperation important? Communication? Clear roles?
8. Why is Tired of Singing upset?
9. What is a compromise?
10. How can Tired of Singing compromise with Marcia?

EXERCISE 10 What Should the People Do?

Read the problems. Answer the questions in your notebook.

1. Usually Sara gets to work early on Tuesdays because the store's order comes in then. This morning, Sara was at work at 7:00 AM, but the order didn't arrive. Sara's coworker, Ben, didn't tell Sara that he changed the delivery day. Is the problem clear roles or communication? How can they fix the problem?
2. Tyrone and Yolanda are custodians in a building. Tyrone washes the floors and Yolanda takes out the trash. This morning, he washed the first floor. Then she took out the trash. Now the floor is a mess, and Tyrone has to wash it again. Is the problem clear roles or cooperation? How can they fix the problem?
3. John and Ted are delivery drivers for a soda company. They like to eat lunch in a restaurant. But John wants to get hamburgers and Ted wants to get tacos. They argue about lunch every day. How can they compromise?

EXERCISE 11 Compromising

A. When people compromise, each person gives up something in order to agree on something that's more important. For example, Diane and Tim are working together on a project. Tim wants to start work on the project every day at 7:00. Diane wants to start work at 9:00. They agree to start work together at 8:00. Look at the chart.

People	What They Agreed On	What They Gave Up
Diane	They agreed to start work at 8:00.	She will start one hour earlier than she wants.
Tim		He will start one hour later than he wants.

How did you solve John and Ted's problem in Exercise 10, item 3? Write a chart in your notebook.

B. Work with a partner. You and your partner work in an office that is open from 7:00 AM to 7:00 PM. One of you has to start work early to open the office, and one of you has to start work late and stay to close the office. But both of you hate getting to work at 7:00 AM. How can you compromise? Write a chart in your notebook.

Reading Journal

Complete a copy of the reading journal form on page 126. Keep the form in your notebook or portfolio.

Taking Action

Teamwork is important at home, at work, and in the community. How do you want to be a better team player? Complete the chart.

Teamwork Skill	What Will You Do?
Communication	
Cooperation	
Clear Roles	

Bridging to the Future

At the start of each new year, many people make lists of things they want to change or improve in their lives. We call these changes **resolutions.** Imagine that today is December 31. What do you want to change or improve in your life? Make a list. Share your list with the class.

Family Connection

People who live together in a home need clear roles. For example, the people should have clear roles about chores. In your home, are there clear roles for doing chores? Who makes the beds, cooks, cleans up, and takes out the trash? Talk to your family about making a list of chores. Assign each person in your family a clear role.

Enriching Your Vocabulary

There are many words we can use for people we work with:

boss	vice president	secretary
manager	president	clerk
supervisor	coworker	salesperson
department head	assistant	

What's your job title? Your boss's? Tell the class.

Review

EXERCISE 12 Answer the Questions

A. Look at the letter to the advice column. What's the main idea? Use the title picture, caption, and first sentence of each paragraph. Write the answer in your notebook.

At Work
by Carla Carson

Noisy Extrovert Causes Problems

DEAR CARLA,

I work in a small office. I work with the office manager and a new employee, Neal. I am having trouble getting along with Neal. Neal is very noisy. He wants to talk while he works. He's always asking questions, telling jokes, and talking about his work.

Sometimes his friends call, and he will talk to them for a few minutes in a loud voice. Neal is a nice person, and he's good at his job. Customers like Neal because he's friendly. I am friendly, too, but I need quiet to do my job. I can't work when Neal is making noise. What can I do?

Signed,
Quiet Delia

B. Write the answers in your notebook.

1. Is Neal an introvert or an extrovert? How do you know?
2. Is Delia an introvert or an extrovert? How do you know?
3. What problems are they having?
4. How can Delia solve the problem?

Your Portfolio

Put a copy of the chart you made in Taking Action on page 12 in your portfolio.

Summing Up

I can:

- ☐ **1.** Take a quiz about personality types.
- ☐ **2.** Read about teamwork skills at work.
- ☐ **3.** Preview a reading before I read.
- ☐ **4.** Understand gerunds.
- ☐ **5.** Use a KWLH chart to help me read.
- ☐ **6.** ____________________

UNIT 2

Around Town

Accessing Information

In this unit, you will:

1. Read about a shopping mall.
2. Read a transportation map and schedule.
3. Use maps and drawings to help you read.
4. Review the present tenses.
5. Use maps and drawings.

Talk About It

Look at the pictures. Where are the people? What are they doing?

You Decide

How do people in your community get around town? What's the best way to get around your town? How do you get around town?

Key Vocabulary

A. In this unit, you will read about places in the community and how to use transportation to get to them. First, think of all the words you know related to transportation.

B. Study the vocabulary.

department store

garage

mall

concert

camping

amusement park

aquarium

bus

train

subway

public transportation

EXERCISE 1 Vocabulary

Where should the people go? Write the word from Key Vocabulary, part B on the line.

1. Pablo wants to show his children fish. ____________________
2. Ingrid wants to park her car. ____________________
3. Maria and Jadwiga love listening to music. ____________________
4. Max wants to buy jeans and new tools. He only wants to go to one store. ____________________
5. Mr. Priscu wants to hike and sleep outdoors. ____________________

EXERCISE 2 Before You Read

When you read a description, it sometimes helps to make a simple drawing as you read. For example, if you are reading about a mall, you might make a simple drawing. If you are reading directions, you might draw a street map to help you. As you read the article on the next page, circle the information you might use to make a simple map.

Where can you shop, see a movie, and go to a wedding?

CD 1 TRACK 3

The Biggest Mall in the World—and Getting Bigger!

Your older son wants to shop for clothes. Your daughter wants to buy a CD. Your younger son wants to play outdoors. And you and your spouse want a nice meal. Where can you go? To the Mall of America!

The Mall of America is the world's largest indoor shopping mall. It's located near Minneapolis, Minnesota. How big is the Mall of America? Here are some statistics:

- More than 30 Boeing 747 airplanes could fit in the building.
- The mall has over 520 stores, including four major department stores.
- The mall has 50 restaurants and 14 movie theaters.
- There is an indoor amusement park in the mall. The amusement park has 30,000 live plants and 400 trees.
- An aquarium with thousands of different kinds of fish is under the amusement park.
- About 12,000 people work at the mall.
- More than 15 bus lines stop at the mall's $2 million transportation center.
- More than 3,000 people have gotten married at the mall. Many of them bought their wedding clothes at the mall, too.

The mall is a square-shaped building. In each corner of the building is a different department store. The amusement park and aquarium are in the center of the mall, and parking garages for more than 15,000 cars are at two ends of the mall.

Over 42 million people visit the mall each year. Some visitors travel from as far away as Europe, South America, or Asia. Over 350 million people have visited the mall since it opened in 1992.

What can you do at the mall? Here are some popular activities:

- Ride the roller coaster in the amusement park.
- Try golf, baseball, basketball, and other sports at the sports store.
- Take a class in one of 16 different subjects at the mall's college.
- Study English and other subjects at the adult school in the mall.

- Get information on camping and other outdoor activities in Minnesota at the Minnesota Store.

Is the Mall of America too big? Not according to the mall. The mall is adding a new building with more shops and restaurants. The mall is also getting a train station.

Reasons people visit the Mall of America

Visit the amusement park	43%
Shop	92%

EXERCISE 3 After You Read

A. Review your answer to Exercise 2 on page 15. What information did you circle?

B. Work with a small group. Use your answer to part A to draw a simple map of the mall.

EXERCISE 4 Answer the Questions

Write the answers in your notebook.

1. How many stores are at the mall? Restaurants? Movie theaters?
2. How many people visit the mall each year?
3. What are three activities families can do at the mall?
4. In your opinion, what's the most unusual thing people can do at the mall? Why do you think so?

LANGUAGE NOTE
Present Tenses

We use the simple present tense to talk about things that are always true.

The mall **has** 50 restaurants.

We use the present progressive tense to talk about things that are happening now.

The mall **is getting** a train station.

We use the present perfect tense to talk about events that happened:

- over time up to the present
- in the past and are important now
- several times in the past

Over 350 million people **have visited** the mall since 1992.
I'**ve been** to the Mall of America five times.

Review the article on page 16. Circle an example of the simple present, the present progressive, and the present perfect tenses.

Teamwork

A. Work with a partner. Student A looks at the information on the reasons people visit the mall on page 16. Student B looks at the information on the reasons people visit the mall on page 122. Ask your partner questions to complete the chart.

Reasons people visit the Mall of America	
Eat	%
See a movie or a show	%

B. Review your answers to part A. Do people do more than one activity at the mall? What's the most popular activity? The least popular activity? Share your answers with the class.

Giving Voice

Talk It Over

A. Do families go to the Mall of America for shopping or for fun? Why do you think so? Talk over your ideas with a small group. Share your ideas with the class.

B. Look at the prices at the Mall of America. Is a visit to the mall cheap or expensive? How can families visit the mall without spending a lot of money? Work with a small group. Write a list of ideas. Share your ideas with the class.

Mall of America

Prices

Admission to the Mall	Free
Amusement Park	All-day pass: $23.95
Individual Rides	$2.25 to $4.50
Aquarium	Children: $7.95, Adults: $13.95
Bus ticket to the mall	$2.00
Concerts	Free
Parking	Free

EXERCISE 5 Family Activities

A. Your friends or family want to do something fun, but you don't want to spend a lot of money. Work with a group. Create a list of fun activities in your community that don't cost a lot of money. Use the telephone book and the Internet to find out more information about the activities. Call or check the Internet to get prices. Write your ideas in your notebook.

B. Share your answers to part A with the class. Use the class's answers to create a class list of inexpensive activities. Include the name of the activity, the place, and the cost.

Accessing Information

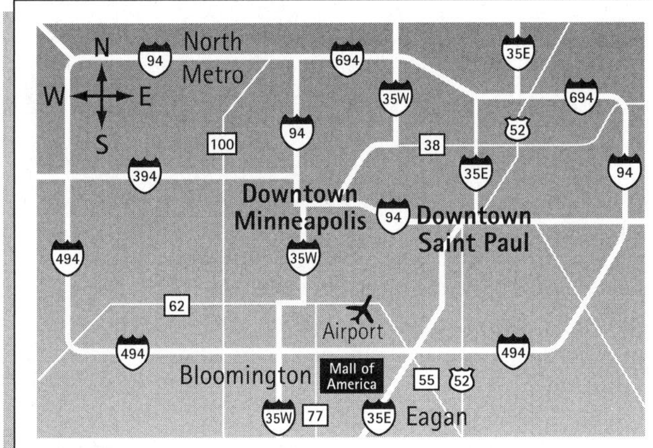

The Mall of America is in Bloomington, Minnesota, on Interstate 494 and Highway 77. The mall is minutes from downtown Minneapolis and St. Paul.

Driving Directions

Take Interstate 494 and use the 24th Street exit.

Public Transportation

From Downtown Minneapolis: Take Express Bus 180. It goes directly to the mall without stopping.

From Downtown St. Paul: Take Bus 54. Bus 54 makes limited stops.

Talk About It

You are in downtown St. Paul. How can you get to the mall? Talk over your ideas with your partner. Share your answers with the class.

You Decide

Do you like to walk, drive, or take the bus or train? Why?

Enriching Your Vocabulary

We use **north, south, east,** and **west** to give directions. We often use N, S, E, and W as abbreviations for these words. Usually, a compass shows north, south, east, and west on the map. North is usually at the top of the map. Circle the compass on the map above.

EXERCISE 6 Using a Map

A. Use the map above. Write **north, south, east,** or **west** on the line.

1. The Mall of America is __________ of downtown Minneapolis.
2. St. Paul is __________ of Minneapolis.
3. To get to St. Paul from the mall, go __________ on highway 35E.

B. Work with a partner. Look at the map above. You live on Highway 52 north of 694. How do you drive to the mall? Write directions in your notebooks. Share your answers with the class.

READING STRATEGY
Use Maps and Drawings to Help You Read

Maps and drawings can help you when you read. As you know, when a reading contains a map or a drawing, you should study it before you read. The map or drawing will help you understand the reading.

Sometimes, a map or a drawing is a main part of the information you are reading. This is the case with bus schedules and driving directions. In this case, study the map and the schedule or directions carefully.

When you are reading a schedule or directions, you only want specific information. You want directions to a specific place. So when you read, pay attention to only the information you need.

Sometimes, a reading has a description of a place, but doesn't have a map or a drawing. In this case, you might make a simple drawing to help you as you read.

EXERCISE 7 Maps and Drawings

What kinds of readings might have a map or a drawing? Check the boxes.

- ☐ **1.** a train schedule
- ☐ **2.** a recipe for soup
- ☐ **3.** an article about places to visit downtown
- ☐ **4.** directions for riding the subway downtown
- ☐ **5.** an article about the president
- ☐ **6.** ______________________________

EXERCISE 8 Before You Read

On pages 21 and 22, you will read a map and a bus schedule. Before you complete the exercises, follow these steps:

1. Look over the map. Circle the compass.

2. Find the bus stops downtown on the map and on the schedule.

STUDY SKILL
Using an Atlas

An atlas is a book of maps. An atlas contains maps of countries around the world or states in the U.S. A road atlas contains road maps. There are other kinds of atlases, too. If possible, visit the library to view different kinds of atlases. You can also get free maps and directions on the Internet. Ask your teacher or a librarian to show you how.

Bus 54 Downtown St. Paul/Mall of America

Monday–Friday Eastbound
from Mall of America
to downtown St. Paul via Airport

route number & letter	Mall of America Transit Center 1	Minneapolis/St. Paul International Airport 2	West 7th St and West Maynard Dr 3	Downtown St. Paul: 5th St and West 7th St 4	Downtown St. Paul: 5th St and Minnesota St 5	Downtown St. Paul: 5th St Layover 7
			AM			
54D	4:31	4:41	4:46	4:57	5:00	5:05
54D	4:59	5:09	5:14	5:25	5:28	5:33
54D	5:24	5:34	5:39	5:50	5:53	5:58
54D	6:00	6:10	6:15	6:26	6:29	6:34
54D	6:21	6:31	6:36	6:47	6:50	6:55
54D	6:54	–	7:06	7:17	7:20	7:25
54D	7:24	–	7:36	7:47	7:50	7:55
54D	7:50	8:00	8:06	8:16	8:20	8:25
54D	8:31	8:41	8:46	8:57	9:01	9:06
54D	9:01	9:11	9:15	9:26	9:20	9:35
54D	9:31	9:41	9:45	9:56	10:00	10:05
54D	10:01	10:11	10:15	10:26	10:30	10:35
54D	10:31	10:41	10:45	10:56	11:00	11:05
54D	11:00	11:10	11:14	11:25	11:29	11:34
54D	11:30	11:40	11:41	11:55	11:59	12:04
			PM			
54D	12:00	12:10	12:14	12:25	12:29	12:34
54D	12:30	12:40	12:44	12:55	12:59	1:04
54D	1:00	1:10	1:14	1:25	1:29	1:34
54D	1:30	1:40	1:44	1:55	1:59	2:04
54D	2:00	2:10	2:14	2:25	2:29	2:34
54D	2:30	2:40	2:45	2:56	3:00	3:05
54D	3:00	3:10	3:15	3:25	3:30	3:35
54D	3:30	3:41	3:46	3:57	4:01	4:07
54D	4:00	4:11	4:16	4:27	4:31	4:37
54D	4:30	4:41	4:46	4:57	5:01	5:07
54D	5:00	5:11	5:16	5:27	5:31	5:37
54D	5:29	5:40	5:45	5:56	6:00	6:06
54D	6:00	6:10	6:15	6:26	6:30	6:35
54D	6:41	6:51	6:58	7:07	7:11	7:16
54D	7:11	7:21	7:26	7:37	7:41	7:16
54D	7:42	7:52	7:56	8:07	8:11	8:16
54D	8:12	8:22	8:26	8:37	8:41	8:46
54D	8:42	8:52	8:56	9:07	9:11	9:16
54D	9:12	9:22	9:26	9:37	9:41	9:46
54D	9:42	9:52	9:56	10:07	10:11	10:16
54D	10:42	10:52	10:56	11:07	11:11	11:16
54D	11:42	11:52	11:56	12:07	12:11	12:16
			AM			
54D	12:42	12:52	12:56	1:07	1:11	1:16

Monday–Friday Westbound
from downtown St. Paul
to Mall of America via Airport

route number & letter	Downtown St. Paul: 5th St Layover 7	Downtown St. Paul: 8th St and Cedar St 6	Downtown St. Paul: West 7th St and 5th St 4	West 7th St and West Maynard Dr 3	Minneapolis/St. Paul International Airport 2	Mall of America Transit Center 1
			AM			
54M	4:22	4:27	4:31	4:43	4:48	4:58
54M	5:11	5:16	5:20	5:32	5:37	5:47
54M	5:41	5:46	5:50	6:02	6:07	6:17
54M	6:11	6:16	6:20	6:32	6:37	6:47
54M	6:41	6:46	6:50	7:02	7:07	7:17
54M	7:11	7:16	7:20	7:32	7:32	7:47
54M	7:42	7:47	7:51	8:03	8:08	8:18
54M	8:12	8:17	8:21	8:33	8:38	8:48
54M	8:42	8:47	8:51	9:03	9:07	9:17
54M	9:12	9:17	9:21	9:33	9:37	9:47
54M	9:42	9:47	9:51	10:03	10:07	10:17
54M	10:12	10:17	10:21	10:33	10:37	10:47
54M	10:42	10:47	10:51	11:03	11:07	11:17
54M	11:12	11:17	11:21	11:33	11:37	11:47
54M	11:42	11:47	11:51	12:03	12:07	12:17
			PM			
54M	12:12	12:17	12:21	12:33	12:37	12:47
54M	12:42	12:47	12:51	1:03	1:07	1:17
54M	1:12	1:17	1:21	1:33	1:37	1:47
54M	1:42	1:47	1:51	2:03	2:07	2:17
54M	2:12	2:17	2:21	2:33	2:37	2:47
54M	2:42	2:47	2:51	3:03	3:07	3:17
54M	3:11	3:17	3:22	3:34	3:39	3:50
54M	3:41	3:47	3:52	4:04	4:09	4:20
54M	4:11	4:17	4:22	4:34	4:39	4:50
54M	4:41	4:47	4:52	5:04	–	5:18
54M	5:11	5:17	5:22	5:34	–	5:48
54M	5:42	5:47	5:51	6:03	6:09	6:19
54M	6:12	6:17	6:21	6:33	6:39	6:48
54M	6:52	6:57	7:01	7:13	7:18	7:28
54M	7:22	7:27	7:31	7:43	7:49	7:58
54M	7:52	7:57	8:01	8:13	8:18	8:28
54M	8:22	8:27	8:31	8:43	8:47	8:57
54M	8:52	8:57	9:01	9:13	9:17	9:27
54M	9:22	9:27	9:31	9:43	9:47	9:57
54M	10:22	10:27	10:31	10:43	10:47	10:57
54M	11:22	11:27	11:31	11:43	11:47	11:57

Shaded times denote rush-hour service.

continued →

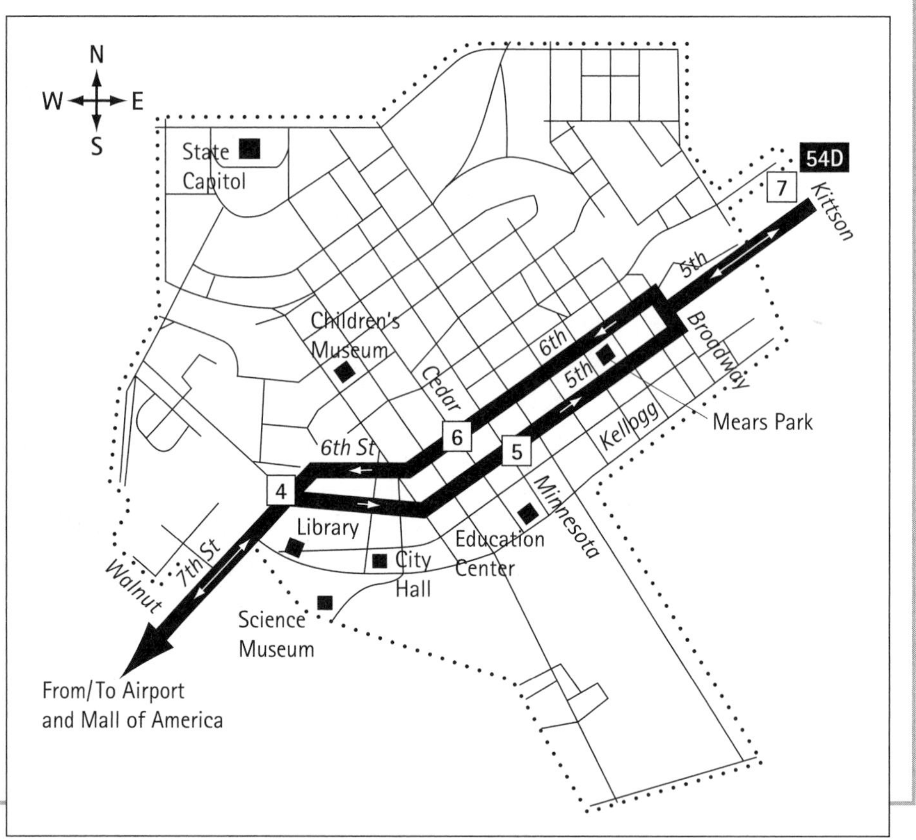

EXERCISE 9 After You Read

A. The people are taking the bus downtown. Help them. Write the stop number on the line.

1. Raul Monte wants to take his nephews to the Children's Museum. __________
2. Sally Cogliano has a job interview at the Education Center. __________
3. Cindy Le is meeting a friend at a restaurant near Mears Park. __________
4. Ira Goldstein needs to go to City Hall. __________
5. Jean Minders needs to return some books to the library. __________

B. Review your answer to Exercise 8 on page 20. Did reviewing the map help you complete the exercise? Tell your partner. Share your ideas with the class.

EXERCISE 10 Which Bus Do They Take?

Use the bus schedule on page 21. Write the time of the bus on the line.

1. Mustafa Rezak has a job interview at the mall at 10:00 AM. He wants to arrive at the mall by 9:30 AM. He's at 8th Street and Cedar Street. __________
2. Lidia Sanchez is the manager of a restaurant at the mall. She leaves work at 9:00 PM and takes bus 54 home. __________
3. Ana Hom and her friends want to take the bus to the mall after school. Their school is near West 7th Street and 5th Street. School ends at 3:30 PM. __________
4. Ted Williams works at the airport. He wants to go shopping at the mall after work. He finishes work at 3:30 PM. __________
5. Alison Hills lives near the mall. She wants to go to the library. She wants to get to the library at about 2:00 PM. __________

EXERCISE 11 Bus Fares

Read the information on bus fares. Then write the fare for each person in Exercise 10. (Today is Friday.)

BUS FARES		
	Rush Hours	Non-Rush Hours
Adults (ages 13 to 64)	$1.75	$1.25
Seniors (Age 65 or older)	$1.75	$0.50
Youth (Ages 6 to 12)	$1.75	$0.50
Exact change required. Children under age 6 ride free with an adult. Rush hours are 6:00 AM to 9:00 AM and 3:30 PM to 6:30 PM, Monday to Friday (except holidays).		

1. Mustafa Rezak is 34 years old. __________
2. Lidia Sanchez is 45 years old. __________
3. Ana Hom is 12 years old. __________
4. Ted Williams is 40 years old. __________
5. Alison Hills is 66 years old. __________

Reading Journal

Complete a copy of the reading journal form on page 126. Keep the completed form in your notebook or portfolio.

Taking Action

A. Look at the list of inexpensive activities you made in Exercise 5 on page 18. How can you get to each one? Car? Bus? Train? Walk? Make a chart in your notebook. Follow the example.

Activity	Method of Transportation
Take children to park	Walk

B. Choose one of the places from part A. How do you get there? Get a bus or train schedule or map. Use the telephone book, library, or Internet to help you. Use the information to make a map and directions from your school to the place. Share your map and directions with the class.

Bridging to the Future

Many people have cars or want to own one. They say that cars are faster and more convenient than public transportation. But cars are also expensive. Work with a group. In your notebook, make a list of the advantages and disadvantages of having a car. Make a list of ways to get an inexpensive car, too. Share your ideas with the class.

Workplace Connection

How do people in your community get to work? How much does it cost? Is each one fast or slow? Make a chart with three columns: **method of transportation, cost,** and **time.** For cost, consider all the costs (gas, parking, fares, insurance, etc.). Use the information you gathered in Taking Action to help you. Then share your results with the class. Which kind of transportation do you use? Why? Do you want to make any changes based on the information you learned?

Review

EXERCISE 12 Using a Schedule

Read the information and answer the questions. Write the answers in your notebook.

The Taste of Chicago

The Taste of Chicago is the city's largest outdoor festival. It takes place downtown. You can try food from over 65 restaurants, listen to live music, and see famous singers.

Take Public Transportation to the Taste of Chicago!

Over 4 million people will go to the Taste of Chicago. Public transportation is the best way to get there. Red line subway trains run every 15 minutes from the north and south sides of Chicago. Blue line trains run from the northwest and west sides of Chicago every 15 minutes. Orange line trains run from the southwest side of Chicago every 20 minutes. Trains run 24 hours a day. The fare is $1.50.

1. What is the Taste of Chicago?
2. Is it a good idea to drive to the Taste of Chicago? Why or why not?
3. Mario and Elena live on the north side of Chicago. Which train line should they take?
4. Jennifer Sang lives on the southwest side of Chicago. Which train line should she take?
5. Ray works at the Taste of Chicago until 12:00 at night. Can he take the subway home?

Your Portfolio

Look at the list of activities you wrote in Exercise 5 on page 18. Put the list in your portfolio.

Summing Up

I can:

- ☐ **1.** Read about a shopping mall.
- ☐ **2.** Read a transportation map and schedule.
- ☐ **3.** Use maps and drawings to help me read.
- ☐ **4.** Review the present tenses.
- ☐ **5.** Use maps and drawings.
- ☐ **6.** ______________________________

Keeping Busy

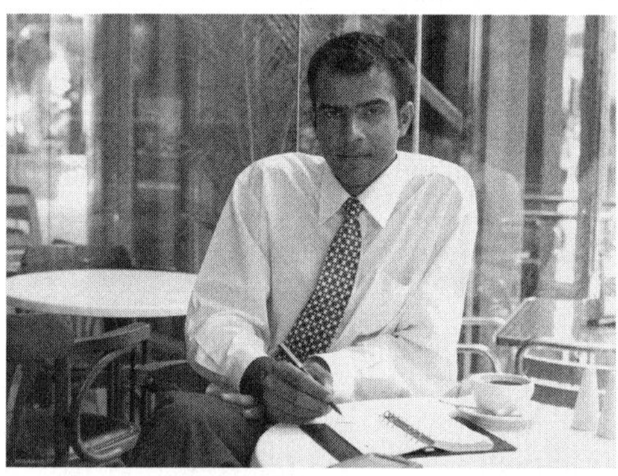

In this unit you will:

1. Read about wedding customs in the U.S. and around the world.
2. Read a time-off policy from work.
3. Read and make judgments.
4. Understand **used to**.
5. Use calendars.

Accessing Information

Talk About It

Where are the people? What are they doing? What are they probably thinking?

You Decide

A friend at work just got married. What do you say? What do you do? Why?

Key Vocabulary

A. In this unit, you will read about wedding customs and time off from work. First, work with a partner. In your notebook, write a list of words you know about reasons people take time off from work. Include weddings. Include other reasons, too.

B. Study the vocabulary.

bride–woman who is getting married

groom–man who is getting married

couple–two adults who are together, either married or dating

culture–things that people from one country think or do

customs–things that people usually do; traditions

reception–the party after a wedding

ceremony–the part of a wedding when the couple gets married

personal day–day off from work to take care of personal business

vacation day–day off from work for fun and relaxation

sick day–day off from work because you're sick

EXERCISE 1 Vocabulary

Write the word from Key Vocabulary, part B on the line.

1. Next summer I'm using five ____________________ to visit my relatives in Mexico.
2. I feel terrible. I need to take a ____________________ to see the doctor.
3. Hong is going to use one ____________________ for an interview for a part-time job on weekends.
4. Most cultures have a lot of special ____________________ for weddings and other special days.
5. People often dance, eat, and drink at a wedding ____________________.

EXERCISE 2 Before You Read

The reading on the next page is about weddings in different cultures. As you read, figure out if weddings take a lot of time. What can couples do to have enough time for their weddings? Write a few ideas in your notebook.

Why is a wedding day special?

CD 1 TRACK 4

Weddings Around the World

In cultures around the world, a wedding is a happy time. Weddings are a time for people to celebrate a new beginning for the bride and groom. However, even though wedding ceremonies have similar purposes, customs are different in different cultures. Here are wedding customs in three cultures.

China

In traditional Chinese weddings, brides used to wear red. But these days, many Chinese brides wear white wedding gowns. However, red is still the color for wrapping gifts and for wedding invitations. On the wedding day, the groom goes to the bride's house. There, he will give presents to the bride and her family, and the couple will serve tea to her parents and older relatives. Then the couple goes to the groom's house and serves his family tea. Next, the couple and the immediate family go to the ceremony. After that, the couple goes to a park or photo studio to take pictures. Finally, everyone meets for the reception. At weddings, people set off fire-crackers to keep away bad luck.

Morocco

A Moroccan wedding lasts several days. Before the wedding begins, the bride and her friends put a special herb called henna on their hands and feet at a party. They make beautiful designs with the herb, which makes the skin turn dark red. The day of the wedding, the bride's friends help her fix her hair and put on a beautiful gown. Brides usually wear beautiful jewelry and a fancy headpiece. Then the groom's family comes to take her to her new home. In the past, the bride used to travel by horse or donkey to her new home. But now most brides travel by car. The drivers always honk their horns loudly. Then the family hosts a party for friends and relatives. At this party a large meal is served.

United States

Because people in the U.S. came from many countries, customs from many countries are part of U.S. weddings. Nevertheless, U.S. weddings have many common features. Before the wedding, a bride's friends may have a party called a shower. At the shower, the friends laugh, play games, and give the bride presents. At the wedding, guests usually give gifts, too. Often couples register with a store so that guests know what silverware, plates, and other things the couple needs. Guests can order one or two items. At the wedding, the bride usually wears a white gown. Many Americans believe that it's bad luck for the groom to see the bride in her wedding gown before the ceremony. The groom usually wears a suit or tuxedo. In the past, ceremonies used to be very traditional. Today, however, some people have unusual weddings. People have gotten married while skydiving, scuba diving, or flying in a balloon. After the ceremony, the family holds a reception for the guests. Food at the reception can range from just wedding cake to a large meal.

Wedding Customs

People think these customs bring good luck.

China People get married at half-past the hour.

Morocco People give the couple special cone-shaped sugar.

Mexico The guests form a heart-shaped ring around the couple as they dance.

EXERCISE 3 After You Read

A. Review your answer to Exercise 2 on page 27. Do weddings take a lot of time? How can couples find the time for their wedding? Share your ideas with the class.

B. You are going to the wedding of a Chinese friend. Money is a good gift for a Chinese wedding, so you want to give the couple some money. What color should the envelope be? Use the information in the article to figure out the answer. Write the color on the line. ______________________

EXERCISE 4 Answer the Questions

Write the answers in your notebook.

1. What color dresses do many Chinese brides wear these days?
2. What color did they use to wear?
3. Why do Chinese people set off firecrackers at weddings?
4. How long do Moroccan weddings last?
5. What do Moroccan brides wear?
6. What color does a U.S. bride often wear?
7. What happens at a wedding shower?
8. What's an example of a nontraditional wedding?

LANGUAGE NOTE
Used To

We use **used to** to talk about things that were habits in the past but don't happen now.

All Chinese brides **used to** wear red.

Did Chinese brides **use to** wear red?

The article on page 28 has three examples of **used to.** Circle them.

Teamwork

A. Work with a partner. Student A looks at the information on wedding customs on page 28. Student B looks at the information on wedding customs on page 122. Complete the chart. Ask, "What do people in (India) do for good luck at a wedding?" Answer your partner's questions.

Country	Good Luck Custom
India	
U.S.	
Japan	

B. Switch roles and repeat the activity.

Giving Voice

Talk It Over

A. Complete the chart. Write about wedding customs in your culture. Have wedding customs changed? Write about what people used to do in the past. Then write about what people do now. (If you are from one of the cultures in the article, give more information about weddings in your culture.)

Wedding Customs in the Past	Wedding Customs Today

B. Work with a partner. Tell your partner about weddings in your culture in the past and today. Listen to your partner. Take notes in your notebook. Then use your notes to tell the class about weddings in your partner's culture.

EXERCISE 5 Wedding Manners

A. Work with a small group. Talk about what U.S. weddings are like. What do people wear, bring, do, and say? Use information from the article. Have you attended a wedding in the U.S. or seen one in a movie or TV program? Share your experiences with the group.

B. Work with your group. Your group is invited to a wedding in the U.S. Prepare a list of tips. Share your list with the class. Use everyone's ideas to prepare a class list.

Tips for Wedding Guests

1. ______________________________
2. ______________________________
3. ______________________________
4. ______________________________
5. ______________________________

Accessing Information

JUNE 15–21		
Sunday, June 15	2:00	Wedding shower for Alana
Monday, June 16		
Tuesday, June 17		
Wednesday, June 18	2:00	Pick up Martin's parents at airport
Thursday, June 19		Pick up wedding gown and bridesmaid's dress
Friday, June 20	6:30 7:30	Wedding rehearsal Rehearsal dinner, Richard's Restaurant
Saturday, June 21	9:00 3:00	Go to hairdresser's with Alana Alana's wedding

JUNE 22–28

Mr. and Mrs. Robert Carter
Request the honor of your presence at
the wedding of their daughter
Alana Jean
to
Mr. Martin Duran
Saturday, June 21 at 3:00 o' clock
Green Gardens Restaurant
Sacramento, California

Talk About It

Rhonda Carter's sister, Alana, is getting married this week, so Rhonda is very busy helping her. Look at Rhonda's calendar and the invitation. What day is the wedding? What time? Where? What other things does Rhonda have to do to get ready?

You Decide

Look at the invitation again. The bride's family is from California, and the groom's family is from Guatemala. What can the families do to make sure everyone feels comfortable at the wedding? Talk over your ideas with a partner. Share your ideas with the class.

READING STRATEGY
Read and Make Judgments

When we read, we use the information in the reading to make judgments. For example, you are going to go to a wedding. You read a book about weddings in the U.S. As you read, you decide that you will give the couple some silverware for a present. Or imagine that you need a day off from work next month for a relative's wedding. You read the company's time-off policy. You find out you have to ask for a day off in advance. So you decide to talk to your boss about the day off right away.

EXERCISE 6 Reading and Making Judgments

When do you read and make judgments? Circle the numbers.

1. You want to see a movie tonight. You are reading about new movies in the newspaper.
2. You're reading a story to your children. The children are enjoying the story.
3. You want to open a bank account. You have information on bank accounts at three banks.
4. It's Sunday morning. You're reading the comics in the Sunday newspaper.

EXERCISE 7 Before You Read

A. An employee handbook gives information on company rules and policies. The reading on the next page is the time-off policy from a company handbook. What time off do *you* need from work for the next two months? Complete the calendar. Write the month and the time off you need.

Month: ______________	Month: ______________

B. As you read the time-off policy on the next page, think about the time off you need from your job. Should you use vacation days or personal days? In the calendar in part A, write V (for vacation day) or P (for personal day) for each day off.

Do you need a day off?

Martin Duran needs some time off from work for his wedding and honeymoon. He works at Torrence Metal Products. Read the time-off policy from Torrence Metal Products.

CD 1 TRACK 5

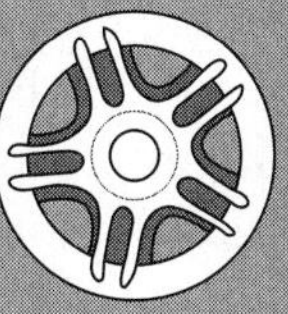

Time-Off Policy

Torrence Metal Products recognizes that its employees need time off for vacation, personal business, and health care. Therefore, all employees of Torrence Metal Products are entitled to these days off.

Vacation Days

All full-time employees of Torrence Metal Products get paid vacation days as follows. Vacation days are awarded on January 1 of each year based on service during the previous year.

Length of Service	Vacation Days a Year
Less than 6 months	1 day of vacation for each complete month of service
6 to 11 months	6 days
1 to 5 years	10 days
6 to 10 years	15 days
11 years or more	20 days

Employees who start after January 1 will get vacation time as follows:
Employees hired between January 2 and June 30 will get 5 days of vacation to be used after they have worked 6 months. Employees hired after June 30 receive no vacation time that year. Employees must use their vacation time in the year they get it. Employees must request vacation time in advance.

Personal Days

Personal days are for conducting personal business, such as buying and selling a home, taking care of legal matters, or other personal business.

Length of Service	Personal Days a Year
Less that 6 months	1 day
More than 6 months	3 days

An employee must request a personal day at least a day in advance. A manager may approve additional personal time off without pay.

Sick Days

Each employee at Torrence Metals is entitled to a reasonable number of paid sick days. If an employee is sick for 3 days or more, a note from the employee's doctor is required. If an employee is sick for 1 or 2 days, no note is required.

continued 

On January 1 of each year, each employee will get 10 sick days for that year. Employees hired after January 1 will get sick days according to the day they start working:

Date Hired	Sick Days a Year
January 1 to June 30	10 days
After June 30	5 days

If an employee is sick for 11 to 30 days, he or she will be covered by company-paid short-term disability insurance. Sicknesses of more than 30 days will be covered by optional long-term disability insurance. All employees are urged to buy long-term disability insurance through the company payroll deduction plan. As with vacation time, employees must use sick days in the year they are earned.

EXERCISE 8 After You Read

Answer the questions. Write the answers in your notebook.

1. Martin worked for the company for five years. He hasn't taken off any days this year. Can he take off six days for his wedding?
2. What does Martin need to do to get the time off?

EXERCISE 9 You're the Boss

These employees want days off. Can the employees take the time off? Write **yes** or **no** in your notebook. Then share your answers with the class. Does everyone agree?

1. Irina Lobo has worked for the company for five months. On Tuesday she asked if she can take a personal day on Thursday to take care of a traffic ticket. There is not a lot of work to do on Thursday.
2. Julia Smith has worked for the company for two years. On Thursday at 4:00 she asked if she can take a vacation day on Friday. She wants to go to an amusement park with her children. She has not taken any vacation days all year. The company is very busy on Friday.
3. Todd Mahootian has worked for the company for two years. He has already taken ten vacation days this year. Now he wants to take six vacation days because his grandparents are visiting him.

Enriching Your Vocabulary

We use many words to talk about insurance. Study the vocabulary.

premium—the money we pay for insurance

claim—when you ask for money from your insurance company, you make a claim

deductible—when you make a claim, the part of the claim you pay

co-pay—small amount you pay for medicine or a doctor's visit

EXERCISE 10 Reminder Calendar

A. A reminder calendar is a special calendar we use to keep track of events that happen every year. We keep the calendar from year to year because it never changes. A reminder calendar is a good place to write down dates such as your wedding anniversary, birthdays of friends and relatives, religious holidays, and other special days.

Look at the reminder calendar that Selena Lopez made. Then answer the questions in your notebook.

January	February *14 Valentine's Day*	March *2 Texas Independence Day*
April *15 pay income taxes*	May	June *23 wedding anniversary*
July *15 Mom and Dad's wedding anniversary*	August	September *1 Brian's birthday*
October	November	December

1. How many special days are on Selena's calendar?
2. What state is Selena probably from? Why do you think so?
3. When is Selena's wedding anniversary?
4. What holiday does Selena celebrate in February?
5. What day are her taxes due?

B. Write the dates in Selena's calendar.

1. Selena's sister's birthday is August 4.
2. Her mother's birthday is December 1.
3. Her father's birthday is February 10.
4. Halloween is October 31.

Reading Journal

Complete a copy of the reading journal form on page 126. Keep the completed form in your notebook or portfolio.

Taking Action

A. When do you need time off from work because of special events in your life? Make a list in your notebook. Talk over your list with a partner. Why are the events important? Tell your partner.

B. What do you need to do and remember every year? Your birthday? Your wedding anniversary? The start of school for your children? Write a reminder calendar for yourself in your notebook. Use your answers to part A. Then share your calendar with the class.

January	February	March
April	May	June
July	August	September
October	November	December

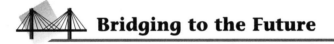

Bridging to the Future

In the U.S., companies are closed on several holidays. However, not all workers celebrate those holidays. Many of these employees celebrate different holidays. They have to use vacation days and personal days for their holidays. Is this fair? What can companies do to make sure that everyone can celebrate important days?

STUDY SKILL
Keeping Track of Important Days

Use your calendar to keep track of important days for work, school, family, and community. Check your calendar every day. That way, you will never miss an important date.

Family Connection

Days off from school are often a problem for parents. Sometimes schools have different holidays than companies. For example, in some places schools celebrate Lincoln's birthday on February 12, but many companies do not. When children have an extra day off, it's a problem for the parents. What can parents do on days like this? Talk over your ideas in a group. Share your ideas with the class.

Review

EXERCISE 11 Reading and Making Judgments

Read the information. Write the answers in your notebook.

Disability Insurance for Employees

Disability insurance is available to all employees to help cover costs when they are unable to work because of sickness or injury.

Short-Term Disability Insurance
This insurance is provided to all employees at company expense. *There is no cost to employees.* Short-term disability insurance pays an employee in case the employee is unable to work for 11 to 30 days.

Long-Term Disability Insurance
This insurance is provided to all employees for a low monthly cost. This insurance pays an employee who is not able to work for more than 30 days.

1. What does short-term disability insurance do?
2. How much does short-term disability insurance cost?
3. What does long-term disability insurance do?
4. How much do employees pay?
5. Is getting long-term disability insurance a good idea? Why do you think so?

Your Portfolio

Look at the list of tips you created in Exercise 5 on page 30. Put a copy of the tips in your portfolio.

Summing Up

I can:

- ☐ **1.** Read about wedding customs in the U.S. and around the world.
- ☐ **2.** Read a time-off policy from work.
- ☐ **3.** Read and make judgments.
- ☐ **4.** Understand **used to.**
- ☐ **5.** Use calendars.
- ☐ **6.** ______________________________

UNIT 4

Money in Your Pocket

In this unit you will:

1. Read about bank accounts.
2. Read about other services that banks offer.
3. Compare and contrast.
4. Use comparative and superlative adjectives.
5. Use a decision matrix.

Accessing Information

Talk About It

Where are the people? What are they doing? What bank services are they using?

You Decide

What can people do at a bank? What do you do at a bank?

Key Vocabulary

A. In this unit, you will read about using the bank. First, work with a partner. In your notebook, write a list of words you know about banks.

B. Study the vocabulary.

withdrawal—money taken out of the bank

deposit—money put in the bank

fee—money you pay for a service

checking account—type of bank account; you keep money in the account and use it by writing a check

savings account—type of bank account; you keep money you don't want to spend right away in the account

loan—money you borrow and then have to pay back

interest—money the bank pays you on the money in your account, or money you pay on a loan

balance—the amount of money you have in the bank

ATM—automated teller machine; machine that lets you make deposits and withdrawals 24 hours a day with a special card from your bank

EXERCISE 1 Vocabulary

What should each person use? Write the word from Key Vocabulary, part B on the line.

1. Wu-sen wants to pay his bills by check. ________________
2. Nadia wants to buy a used car. She wants to get some money and then pay some of it back every month.

   ____
3. It's Saturday night. Byron wants to make a small withdrawal to take his family out for dinner. ________________
4. Gregorio wants to save money for a new car. He wants to keep the money where it's safe. He doesn't want to spend the money. ________________

EXERCISE 2 Before You Read

When you compare and contrast, you talk about ways that two items are the same and different. As you read the article on page 40, pay attention to the ways checking accounts and savings accounts are the same and ways they are different.

How do you open a bank account?

Tarik and Latifa Al-Baghdadi want to open a bank account at North Side Community Bank. They read this brochure to help them choose the best account for their family.

CD 1 TRACK 6

North Side Community Bank

North Side Community Bank has checking and savings plans to meet your needs.

Checking

With a checking account, your money is handy. You can use it to write checks and to pay bills. And because your money is in the bank, it's safe.

☑ Regular Checking

With a regular checking account, you don't have to keep a minimum balance. You pay a monthly fee and a fee if you write more than 10 checks a month.

Minimum balance: none
Monthly service fee: $2.00
Number of free checks per month: 10
(After 10 checks, you pay $0.25 per check.)

☑ Free Checking

Free checking is for customers who want to avoid fees. You have to keep a minimum balance in your account, but you don't have to pay a monthly fee.

Minimum balance: $500.00
Monthly service fee: none
Number of free checks per month: 25
(After 25 checks, you pay $.10 per check.)
Monthly fee if below minimum balance: $3.00

☑ Interest Checking

With interest checking, you have to keep more money in your account, but you get interest on your balance. Interest checking is for customers who want to keep a high balance in their checking accounts and earn interest on their money.

Minimum balance: $1,000.00
Monthly service fee: none
Number of free checks per month: unlimited
Monthly fee if below minimum balance: $4.00
Interest: 1%

Savings

Keep your money safe in a savings account. We have two savings account plans:

☑ Regular Savings

You can start a regular savings account with a low balance and earn interest on your balance.

Minimum balance: $100.00
Monthly service fee: none
Monthly fee if below minimum balance: $3.00
Number of withdrawals per month: 3
Interest: 1%

☑ Golden Savings

With Golden Savings, you have to keep more money in your account, but you get higher interest.

Minimum balance: $1,000.00
Monthly service fee: none
Monthly fee if below minimum balance: $5.00
Number of withdrawals per month: 6
Interest: 2%

EXERCISE 3 After You Read

A. Review your answers to Exercise 2 on page 39. How are savings accounts and checking accounts different? The same? Write a few sentences in your notebook.

B. When you scan, you look for a specific piece of information, such as a name, a number, or something else. You don't read every word. You only look for the information you want. Scan the reading on page 40 for this information.

1. How many checking accounts does the bank offer?
2. Which checking account has the lowest minimum balance?
3. Which checking account pays interest?
4. How many savings accounts does the bank offer?
5. Which has a lower minimum balance, Regular Savings or Golden Savings?

EXERCISE 4 Using a Decision Matrix

A decision matrix is a way to organize information to make decisions. For example, how do you pick the best savings account for you? Look at the decision matrix.

Savings Account Name	Minimum balance	Monthly fee if under minimum	Number of withdrawals per month	Interest
Regular Savings	$100.00	$3.00	3	1%
Golden Savings	$1,000.00	$5.00	6	2%

Now you can compare the information easily. You can only put $300 in the bank right now. So you get Regular Savings.

You want to open a checking account. Write a decision matrix in your notebook. Follow the example above.

Teamwork

Work with a partner. Student A works at the bank. Student B is a customer. Student B wants to open an account. Student B looks at the information on page 123 and tells Student A about his or her needs. Student A uses the information in Exercise 4 and recommends an account. Student B writes the answers in his or her notebook. Then switch roles and repeat the activity.

Giving Voice

Talk It Over

A. What are the advantages of using a bank? The disadvantages? Work with a group. Write a chart in your notebook. Follow the example.

Advantages	*Disadvantages*

B. Share your ideas with the class. Use everyone's ideas to create a class chart. Then discuss the information. Is opening a bank account a good idea? Why or why not?

EXERCISE 5 Opening a Bank Account

You are ready to open an account at North Side Community Bank. Complete the application for an account.

North Side Community Bank

Application for an Account

☐ Checking ☐ Savings

Account type:______________________________

Name:______________________________

Social Security or ID Number:______________________________

LANGUAGE NOTE
Comparative and Superlative Adjectives

We use the comparative form of adjectives to compare two things:

Golden Savings has **higher** monthly fees than Regular Savings.

Regular Checking is **more expensive** than Interest Checking.

We use superlatives to compare three or more things:

Interest checking has the **lowest** fees of all the accounts.

North Community Bank is the **most important** bank in the city.

Some adjectives have irregular forms.

adjective	**comparative**	**superlative**
good	better	best
bad	worse	worst

Review the brochure on page 40. Then take turns comparing the accounts. Use comparative and superlative adjectives.

Accessing Information

North Side Community Bank
Instructions for Writing a Check

501

Pablo Torres
1130 W. Maple Street
Los Angeles, CA 91441

① Date September 8, 2004

③ $37.64

② Pay to the order of: City Electric Company

④ Thirty-seven and 64/100 Dollars

North Side Community Bank
3639 N. Green Street
Los Angeles, CA 91440

⑤ Pablo Torres

264531123: 04563 00501

1. Write the date of the check.
2. Who is the check for? Write the name of the person or company.
3. Write the amount of money in numbers.
4. Write the amount of money in words.
5. Sign your name.

Talk About It

How do you write a check? Point to the check and tell your partner.

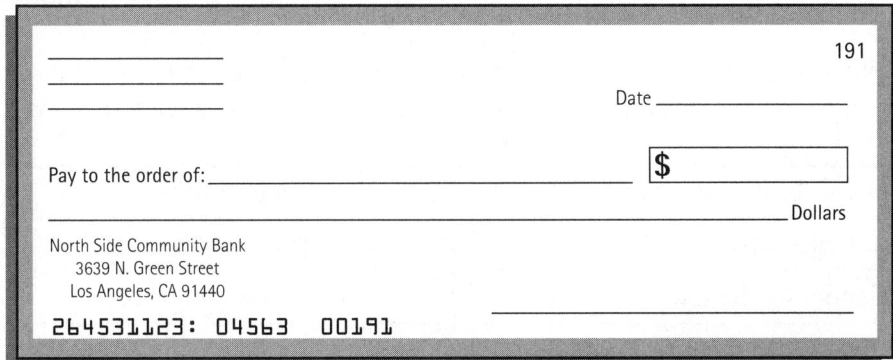
191

Date

Pay to the order of: $

Dollars

North Side Community Bank
3639 N. Green Street
Los Angeles, CA 91440

264531123: 04563 00191

You Decide

Pay the electric bill. Use the blank check.

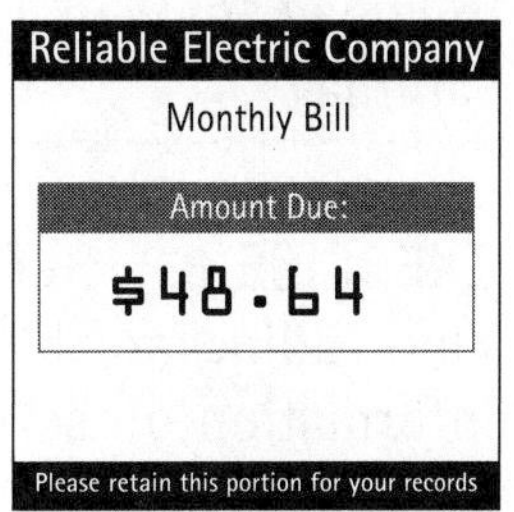
Reliable Electric Company
Monthly Bill
Amount Due:
$48.64
Please retain this portion for your records

READING STRATEGY
Compare and Contrast

When we read, we often compare and contrast the information in the reading.

When you compare, you show how things are the same:

North Side Community Bank is as large as Downtown Bank.

Both banks are large.

When you contrast, you show how things are different:

Interest rates are higher at North Side Community Bank than at Downtown Bank.

Exercise 6 Comparing and Contrasting

A. When do you compare and contrast? Check the boxes.

☐ **1.** You are reading the help wanted ads in the newspaper. You see a job that really interests you.

☐ **2.** You are reading supermarket ads. You notice that bananas are on sale at Greatway. They aren't on sale at Food City.

☐ **3.** You want to open a bank account. You have information on accounts at three different banks.

☐ **4.** It's Tuesday night. You are reading a story to your children.

B. When do you compare and contrast when you read? Tell your partner. Then tell the class.

EXERCISE 7 Decision Matrix

A decision matrix can help you compare and contrast. Look at the decision matrix for two banks. Which bank do you want to use? Why? Work with a partner. Compare and contrast the banks. Write a few sentences in your notebook. Share your sentences with the class.

	North Side Community Bank	Uptown Savings Bank
Location	one block from my house	two blocks from my house
Checking Account	Good—low balance, low fees	Bad—high balance, high fees
Hours	Open 9 AM to 6 PM Monday to Friday, 9 AM to 1 PM Saturday	Open 9 AM to 3 PM Monday to Friday Closed Saturday

EXERCISE 8 Before You Read

The reading on the next page is a brochure from a bank. It gives information on services at the bank. As you read the article, compare and contrast an ATM card and a debit card.

What services does the bank offer?

Linda Borowski is a new employee at North Side Community Bank. She's learning about the bank's services so she can help customers. Read the information.

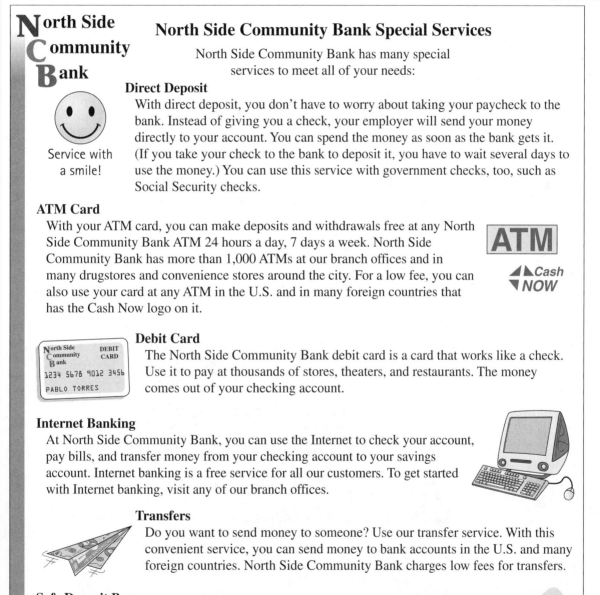

CD 1 TRACK 7

North Side Community Bank

Service with a smile!

North Side Community Bank Special Services

North Side Community Bank has many special services to meet all of your needs:

Direct Deposit

With direct deposit, you don't have to worry about taking your paycheck to the bank. Instead of giving you a check, your employer will send your money directly to your account. You can spend the money as soon as the bank gets it. (If you take your check to the bank to deposit it, you have to wait several days to use the money.) You can use this service with government checks, too, such as Social Security checks.

ATM Card

With your ATM card, you can make deposits and withdrawals free at any North Side Community Bank ATM 24 hours a day, 7 days a week. North Side Community Bank has more than 1,000 ATMs at our branch offices and in many drugstores and convenience stores around the city. For a low fee, you can also use your card at any ATM in the U.S. and in many foreign countries that has the Cash Now logo on it.

North Side
Community
Bank
DEBIT
CARD
1234 5678 9012 3456
PABLO TORRES

Debit Card

The North Side Community Bank debit card is a card that works like a check. Use it to pay at thousands of stores, theaters, and restaurants. The money comes out of your checking account.

Internet Banking

At North Side Community Bank, you can use the Internet to check your account, pay bills, and transfer money from your checking account to your savings account. Internet banking is a free service for all our customers. To get started with Internet banking, visit any of our branch offices.

Transfers

Do you want to send money to someone? Use our transfer service. With this convenient service, you can send money to bank accounts in the U.S. and many foreign countries. North Side Community Bank charges low fees for transfers.

Safe Deposit Boxes

Keep important papers, valuable jewelry, expensive watches, and other items you want to keep safe in one of our safe deposit boxes. Our safe deposit boxes start at $25 per year. We have several sizes of safe deposit boxes for all your needs.

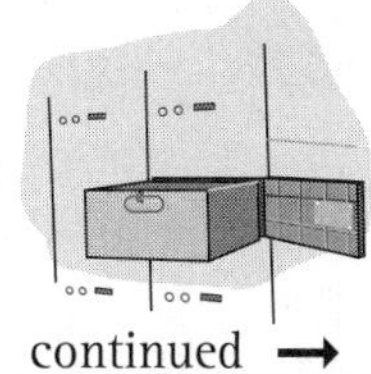

continued →

Car Loans

Are you buying a car? We offer loans on new and used cars. See our experts for a low interest rate.

Credit Card

Do you want a credit card? All North Side Community Bank customers can apply for a credit card that can be used in stores and restaurants nationwide and around the world. You receive a bill each month, and if you pay the full balance on time, you don't pay any interest.

FDIC Insurance

All savings and checking accounts at North Side Community Bank are insured for up to $100,000. That means that if our bank closes, the Federal Deposit Insurance Corporation will pay you the full value of your account, up to $100,000. Your money is always safe at North Side Community Bank.

EXERCISE 9 After You Read

A. Review your answers to Exercise 8 on page 44. How are the cards different? Similar? Share your answers with the class.

B. Write the answers in your notebook.

1. What is direct deposit?
2. When can you use an ATM card?
3. Where can you keep important papers?
4. Can you use a loan to buy a used car?
5. When do people with credit cards have to pay interest?
6. How many ATMs does the bank have?
7. How much does it cost to use an ATM from North Side Community Bank?
8. You are visiting another city. You want to use an ATM. How do you know if you can use your ATM card?
9. Can you transfer money to foreign countries?
10. How do you know your money is safe at the bank?

STUDY SKILL
Using a Decision Matrix

Using a decision matrix is a good way to organize information when you are studying. For example, you are reading about the number of people who need jobs. The article has information on the number of people who have needed jobs the last few years. You want to know if the problem is getting better or worse. So you make a decision matrix of years and people who have needed jobs. Then you can decide if the number of people is going up or down.

EXERCISE 10 Help the Customers

You work at the bank. What do the customers need? Write the letter of the service on the line.

___a___ 1. Mrs. Lopez gets a Social Security check each month. She doesn't like to go to the bank to deposit it.

________ 2. Tuyet doesn't have time to go to the bank. She loves using her computer.

________ 3. Mr. Larson doesn't like to take cash to the supermarket and doesn't want to pay with a credit card.

________ 4. Andrea Blanco wants to send money to her relatives in Florida.

________ 5. Ana has a lot of expensive jewelry. She doesn't want to keep the jewelry at home.

a. direct deposit
b. ATM card
c. debit card
d. Internet banking
e. transfer
f. safe deposit box
g. car loan
h. FDIC insurance

EXERCISE 11 Decision Matrix

A. North Side Community Bank offers ATM cards, debit cards, and credit cards. How are they different? Complete the decision matrix. Write yes or no in the boxes.

Feature	ATM Card	Debit Card	Credit Card
You can withdraw cash and make deposits.	yes	no	no
You can buy things at stores.			
When you buy something, you pay right away from your checking account.			
You pay at the end of the month.			
You may have to pay interest.			

B. You want a card so you can buy things. You don't want to pay interest. You want to pay for the things right away. Which card do you get? ____________________

Reading Journal

Complete a copy of the reading journal form on page 126. Keep the form in your notebook or portfolio.

Taking Action

A. You want to open a bank account. Do you want a checking or savings account? Do you want interest? Low fees? Make a list. Share your list with a partner. Check your partner's list.

B. Work with a small group. Find the names of three or four banks in your area. Visit the banks or use the Internet to get information about accounts at the banks. Use the information to make a decision matrix. Then decide which bank has the best checking or savings account for you. Explain your choice in a few sentences. Show your decision matrix to the class and read your sentences.

Bridging to the Future

Everyone should have some savings. We can use the money in an emergency. We can also use the money to make a large purchase, such as a car. But it's hard to save money. How can you save money? What will you use the money for? Tell your partner. Share your partner's answer with the class.

Community Connection

Banks are private businesses that provide important community services. Other community services are public, such as the post office. Work in two groups. One group makes a list of private organizations that provide community services. The other group makes a list of public organizations that provide community services. Share your list with the other group. Can you add any ideas to the other group's list?

Enriching Your Vocabulary

Banks have many fees. Study the vocabulary.

transfer fee–fee you pay to transfer money

bounced check fee–fee for writing a check for more than the money in your account.

NSF fee–same as bounced check fee; NSF means "not sufficient funds"

Work with a group. Make a list of more bank fees. Share your list with the class.

Review

EXERCISE 12 Answer the Questions

Write the answers in your notebook.

Life Savings Bank Checking Accounts

Economy Checking

Minimum balance: none

Monthly fee: $1.00

Number of free checks: 10 (After 10 checks, you pay $0.10 per check.)

ATM fee: 10 free deposits or withdrawals at Life Savings ATMs. (After 10, each deposit or withdrawal is $1.00. At other ATMs, $1.50.)

Regular Checking

Minimum balance: $500

Monthly fee if below minimum balance: $3.00

Number of free checks: unlimited

ATM fee: None at Life Savings ATMs. At other ATMs, $1.50.

At Life Savings Bank, all checking account customers can get a free debit card.

1. What is the minimum balance for Economy Checking?
2. You have Economy Checking. You made 14 ATM withdrawals this month at Life Savings ATMs. How much will you pay in ATM fees?
3. You have Regular Checking. This month your lowest balance was $498. Will you pay a fee this month? How much?
4. You have Regular Checking. You wrote 11 checks this month. Will you pay a fee for the checks?
5. Can customers get free debit cards at Life Savings?

Your Portfolio

Review the decision matrix you made and sentences you wrote in Taking Action on page 48. Put a copy of the decision matrix and your sentences in your portfolio.

Summing Up

I can:

- ☐ **1.** Read about bank accounts.
- ☐ **2.** Read about other services that banks offer.
- ☐ **3.** Compare and contrast.
- ☐ **4.** Use comparative and superlative adjectives.
- ☐ **5.** Use a decision matrix.
- ☐ **6.** ______________________________

UNIT 5

Taking Care of Yourself

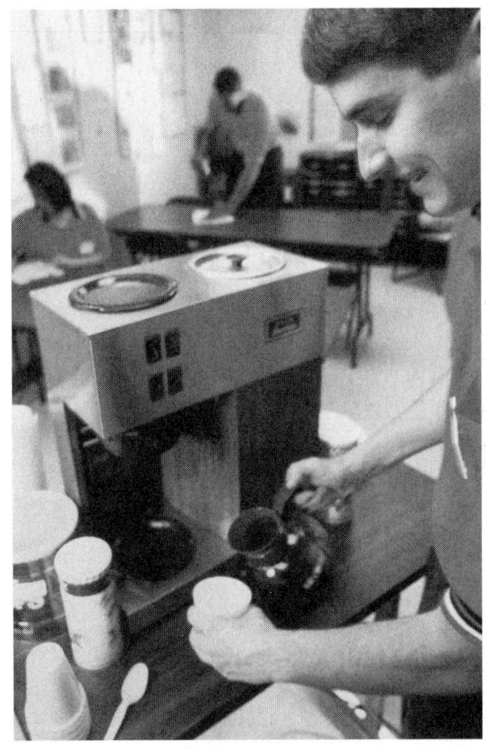

Accessing Information

In this unit, you will:

1. Read about caffeine.
2. Read about getting enough rest.
3. Distinguish between main idea, points, and subpoints.
4. Understand the prefix **over-**.
5. Use clustering.

Talk About It

Where are the people? What are they doing? Is it good for their health?

You Decide

Do you drink coffee or tea? When? Why do you drink it? Do you drink it on breaks at work?

Key Vocabulary

A. In this unit, you will read about caffeine (which is found in coffee, tea, and many other foods and drinks) and about staying safe at work. First, work with a partner. In your notebook, write a list of words related to caffeine. What foods and drinks have caffeine? What does caffeine do to us?

B. Study the vocabulary.

alert–awake; not tired or sleepy

caffeine–it's in coffee and other drinks; it makes us stay awake

decaffeinated–not having caffeine

products–things we buy

pregnant–going to have a baby

habit–something we usually do

habit-forming–something that's hard to stop, such as smoking

cut down on–lower your use of something

break–short time of rest while you are working

avoid–stay away from something

EXERCISE 1 Vocabulary

Write the word from Key Vocabulary, part B on the line.

1. Coffee and tea can be ________________.
2. We've been driving since 5:00 this morning. We need to take a short ________________ to get some rest.
3. Ted drinks eight cups of coffee a day. That's too much! He needs to ________________ coffee.
4. Coffee has ________________ in it.
5. If you can't sleep at night because of coffee, you should try to ________________ coffee at night. Don't drink it after 6:00 PM.

EXERCISE 2 Before You Read

The main idea is what an article is generally about. A detail supports, or backs up, the main idea. As you read the article on page 52, try to figure out the main idea and the details. Write the main idea and two details on the lines.

Main idea: ____

Details: ____

____

Is caffeine bad for us?

CD 1 TRACK 8

Caffeine and Your Health

What do all these products have in common? Nothing, you say? Think again: they all contain the chemical caffeine.

Caffeine is in many foods and drinks. More than 60 plants, including coffee beans, tea leaves, and cocoa beans (the source of chocolate), have caffeine. In addition, companies add it to some drinks. Many kinds of soda have caffeine. But now companies are putting caffeine in more products. For example, new kinds of mineral water and juice have caffeine.

As a result, caffeine consumption is very high. People in the U.S. are spending more time in cafes and coffee shops. And around the world, 80% of adults eat or drink products with caffeine every day. In one recent year, coffee consumption in the U.S. went up 37%.

The Effects of Caffeine

When we eat or drink caffeine, it wakes us up and makes our hearts work a little faster. Caffeine also helps aspirin work faster, and it helps stop some headaches.

However, caffeine has some bad effects. If we have it at night, we may not be able to sleep. Too much caffeine can make us feel angry or upset. Many doctors say that caffeine is not good for children or women who are pregnant. If people eat or drink a large amount of caffeine, their hearts will start working too fast.

In addition to all these effects, caffeine is habit-forming. Just like cigarettes, after people start drinking caffeine, stopping can be very difficult. Also, after people start drinking caffeine, they want more and more. A little caffeine is not bad for most adults. But people should cut down on caffeine if they are getting too much.

Cutting Down on Caffeine

Cutting down on caffeine is not easy, but these tips can help you:

- Caffeine is in more and more products. So check labels carefully.
- Try to drink only two to three cups of coffee, tea, or cola a day.
- Don't stop suddenly. Try to cut down by about a half a cup per day.
- Try decaffeinated coffee or tea. (But keep in mind that even these drinks have a little caffeine.)

Caffeine Content of Common Foods and Drinks

Cup of coffee 135 mg.	Coffee yogurt 45 mg.
Chocolate bar 10 mg.	Diet cola 45 mg.

EXERCISE 3 After You Read

Review your answers to Exercise 2 on page 51. Does everyone agree about the article's main idea? Did everyone find the same details? Use everyone's answers to create a class list of details that support the main idea of the reading.

EXERCISE 4 Answer the Questions

Write the answers in your notebook.

1. What is caffeine?
2. Where do we find caffeine?
3. What are the effects of caffeine?
4. When is caffeine bad for us?
5. Is cutting down on caffeine easy? Why?

EXERCISE 5 Causes and Effects

What's the cause and the effect in each sentence? Circle **C** for **cause** or **E** for **effect**.

1. Our hearts work more quickly **(C/E)** when we drink caffeine **(C/E)**.
2. Caffeine is habit-forming **(C/E)**, so people want to get more and more of it **(C/E)**.
3. Caffeine is in many products now **(C/E)**, so people get more caffeine now than in the past **(C/E)**.
4. Companies are putting caffeine in more products than before **(C/E)** because people like its effects **(C/E)**.

Teamwork

Work with a partner. Student A looks at the information on caffeine content on page 52. Student B looks at the information on caffeine content on page 123. Ask your partner questions and complete the chart. Then switch roles and repeat the activity.

Food	Caffeine Content
Cup of tea	
Caffeinated water	
Decaffeinated coffee	
Cola	

Giving Voice

EXERCISE 6 Product Labels

A. The labels on food packages give important information on what's in food. Look at the product labels. Then answer the questions. Write the answers in your notebook.

Pure *juice*

Ingredients:
100% pure apple juice, vitamin C.
No caffeine.

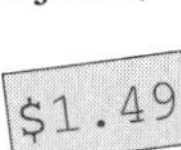

Jump Up
Apple Juice Drink

Ingredients:
Apple juice, water, sugar, artificial color, artificial flavor, caffeine.

1. Which drink is 100% juice?
2. Which drink has caffeine?
3. Which drink has artificial colors and flavors?
4. Which drink has extra vitamin C?
5. Which drink is more expensive?

B. Some people say that added caffeine and artificial flavors and colors are bad for us. They say we should eat and drink natural products. Do you agree? Which drink do you want to buy? Why? Tell your partner. Share your partner's idea with the class.

Enriching Your Vocabulary

Many words are on product labels. Study the vocabulary.

vitamins–vitamins are in foods; vitamins keep us healthy

carbohydrates–bread, rice, and noodles are carbohydrates

protein–meat, fish, and beans have a lot of protein

sodium–salt

saturated fat–fat that is high in cholesterol. A lot of cholesterol is bad for our hearts.

unsaturated fat–fat that is low in cholesterol

Study the label of a food product you like. Find the words on the label. Share your label with the class.

Accessing Information

**The Coffee Break:
The History of a Tradition**

The coffee break is an important workplace tradition. Many companies offer coffee to their employees free or at low cost. At construction sites, coffee wagons (trucks with kitchens) often drive up and sell coffee, snacks, and food. But how did this tradition get started?

Some people say that two companies in Buffalo, New York, started this tradition in about 1902. At that time, factory work was longer and harder than today. In order to help workers, one of the companies began giving workers time to stop work for a few minutes in the morning and the afternoon. Employees used the time to drink coffee. At about the same time, another Buffalo company began to give workers free coffee. Companies noticed that employees worked faster and better when they got regular breaks. So more companies began to offer coffee breaks. Government became involved too: new laws were passed requiring companies to give their employees regular breaks.

Nowadays, the coffee break is a part of most workers' daily routines. Even astronauts take coffee breaks! But employees use this time for many things. They call their children, check their voice mail, or take short walks. And they eat and drink many things—not just coffee! But coffee is such an important part of the culture that we still call this time "coffee break."

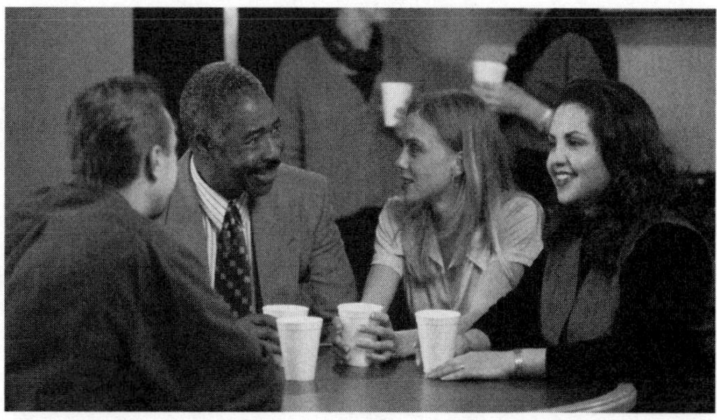

Talk About It

Why do companies like coffee breaks? Why do workers like them? What do they use them for? Do they help employees work better?

You Decide

What do you do on your breaks? Why? Do you drink coffee or something else? Do your breaks help you relax?

READING STRATEGY
Distinguish Between Main Idea, Points, and Subpoints

As you know, a reading has a main idea and details. The **main idea** is general and the details are specific. We call these details **points.** In addition, some details are very specific. These ideas back up, or support, only one point. We call these very specific details **subpoints.** For example, look at these sentences:

Main idea: The coffee break is an important tradition.

Point: Two companies began the tradition in 1902.

Subpoint: One company gave workers short breaks every day.

Subpoint: Another company gave workers free coffee every day.

EXERCISE 7 Points and Subpoints

A. A good way to show the main idea, points, and subpoints is with clustering. When you cluster, you put the main idea in a circle in the center of the graphic organizer. Circles next to that circle contain the points. Then circles connected to those circles have the subpoints.

Look at the information in the cluster. What are the main idea, the point, and the subpoints? Write main idea, point, and subpoint next to the correct circles.

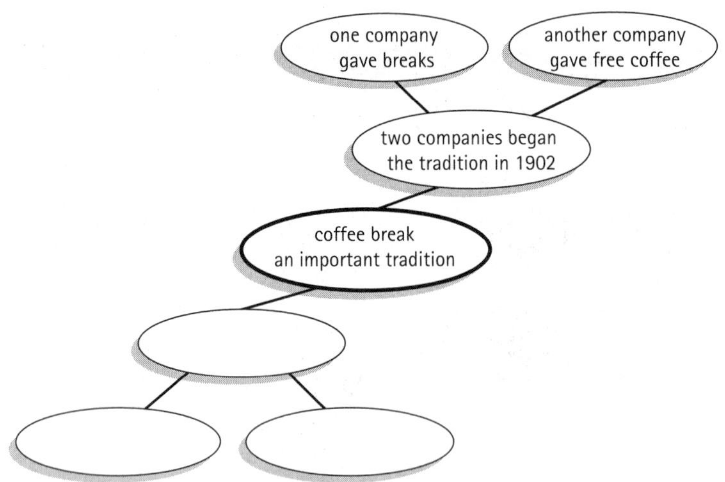

B. Which sentences are points? Subpoints? Write the letters in the correct part of the cluster.

a. Employees use this time for many things.

b. Now the coffee break is part of most workers' daily routine.

c. Employees eat and drink many things besides coffee.

EXERCISE 8 Before You Read

The main idea is what an article is generally about. A detail supports, or backs up, the main idea. As you read the article on pages 57 and 58, try to figure out the main idea and the details. Write the main idea of the article, and the points and subpoints of the first three paragraphs in your notebook.

Are you getting enough sleep?

CD 1 TRACK 9

Get the Rest You Need

Jose Garcia was in a hurry to get to Milwaukee and back—too big a hurry. Jose was a driver for a moving company. He and his assistant, Miguel Rojas, wanted to make two deliveries and go home to Miami before Thanksgiving. They left Jacksonville, Florida, with a customer's furniture and drove to Milwaukee. After unloading there, they picked up a new load of furniture and started to drive back to Florida. They had just enough time to drive to Jacksonville, unload the furniture, and get to Miami for the holiday.

Before they left Milwaukee, Jose felt sleepy, so he drank two cups of coffee. He stopped for more coffee along the way. But Jose and Miguel didn't make it to Florida on time. Jose was so tired that he fell asleep at the wheel. He only fell asleep for a few seconds, but his truck left the road. No one was hurt, but the truck was damaged. And because they had to repair their truck, Jose and Miguel missed Thanksgiving at home.

Jose and Miguel are just one example of workers who were in accidents that were caused by fatigue—overwork or lack of rest. According to government statistics, about 80% of work-related driving accidents involve tired or sleepy drivers. But fatigue also causes many other work accidents. In fact, tired or sleepy workers are at much higher risk of having an accident or injury than workers who get regular rest. Most people need from seven to ten hours of sleep every 24 hours. However, according to reports, more and more people are not getting enough sleep. A recent survey showed that 65% of people said that they don't get enough sleep. In addition to sleep, we also need time off from work to do other things. If we overwork and don't relax, we will feel tired and stressed.

continued →

Are you getting enough rest?

Take the quiz. Circle **yes** or **no.**

1.	Do you get less than seven hours of sleep every 24 hours?	yes	no
2.	Do you work more than 12 hours a day?	yes	no
3.	Do you ever work changing shifts or have irregular hours?	yes	no
4.	Do you ever work a night shift?	yes	no
5.	Do you ever find yourself falling asleep while working or driving?	yes	no
6.	Do you have trouble staying awake when reading or watching TV?	yes	no

If you answered **yes** to more than one question, you need to make sure that you get enough rest. Here are some tips:

1. Keep track of your time. Do important tasks first. Then you won't have to stay up late to take care of them.
2. Try to sleep for eight hours in every 24-hour day. Try to sleep for eight hours at a time. If you can't, try to take a nap during the day.
3. Try to go to bed and get up at the same time every day.
4. Avoid overworking. Try to have at least one day off from work each week.

5. Take regular breaks. In an eight-hour day, workers should take two short breaks, plus a meal break. Avoid foods that make you feel sleepy.
6. Avoid working or driving at times when you are normally asleep.
7. Regular exercise lowers fatigue. Try to exercise at least three days a week.
8. Avoid a lot of caffeine. A little caffeine will wake you up, but a lot of it every day will make you more tired.

If you try these tips and still feel tired or have trouble staying awake, see a doctor. You may have a medical problem.

EXERCISE 9 After You Read

Use the ideas you gathered in Exercise 8 to cluster the ideas in the first two paragraphs of the reading on pages 57 and 58.

EXERCISE 10 Answer the Questions

Write the answers in your notebook.

1. Why did Jose Garcia and Miguel Rojas have an accident?
2. What is fatigue? What causes it?
3. How much sleep should people get every night? Are people getting that much sleep? How do you know?
4. What should people do if they can't sleep for eight hours at a time?
5. What happens when people use a lot of caffeine?

EXERCISE 11 Help the People

A. Are the people getting enough rest? Write **yes** or **no** on the line.

________ **1.** Frank Feng is a student at a community college. He goes to school in the morning and works in the afternoon. After dinner he watches TV and plays video games until 11:00 PM. Then he starts to study. He has trouble staying awake in his classes.

________ **2.** Margarita has a new baby. The baby wakes up every night and cries. Margarita has to stay with the baby until the baby goes back to sleep. She feels tired the next day.

________ **3.** Atur is a clerk at a bank downtown. He works from 8:00 AM to 4:00 PM. His days off are Sunday and Monday. After work, Atur helps his children with their homework, exercises, and reads.

B. Work with a partner. Review your answers to part A. Which people aren't getting enough rest? Write some advice for them in your notebook.

LANGUAGE NOTE
The Prefix *Over-*

The prefix **over-** is very common in English. It means "too much" or "a lot." For example, when we overeat, we eat too much food. We use **over-** to form words such as:

overeat	overuse
overspend	oversleep

What words with **over-** are in the reading on pages 57 and 58? Circle them.

Reading Journal

Complete a copy of the reading journal form on page 126. Put the form in your notebook or portfolio.

Taking Action

A. How many hours do you sleep each night? Complete the chart.

Day	Hours of Sleep
Monday	
Tuesday	
Wednesday	
Thursday	
Friday	
Saturday	
Sunday	

B. Are you getting enough rest? Why do you think so? If you're not getting enough rest, what do you need to do to get more rest? Do you need to make any other changes? For example, do you need to get to bed earlier? Or do you need to go to bed at the same time every night? In your notebook, write a few sentences.

Bridging to the Future

You want to improve your health. What do you want to do? Cut down on caffeine? Get more exercise? Get more rest? Eat more natural foods? Make a list of two or three changes you will make. Share your list with the class.

STUDY SKILL
Staying Alert

Studying is hard work, especially for working adults. A little coffee or caffeinated soda can help you stay awake while you study. But try not to get too much. Try drinking juice, doing some exercises, or getting a little fresh air if you feel tired or sleepy.

Community Connection

Drinking coffee is a social custom around the world. Work with a group. Investigate differences in how people make and drink coffee in the U.S. and in another culture. How do people prepare coffee? What do they put in it? When do they drink it? Where do they drink it? If possible, visit a café or other place where coffee is sold in the U.S. Then compare and contrast your experience with cafés in other countries.

Review

EXERCISE 12 Answer the Questions

Write the answers in your notebook.

Green Tea

Green tea, which people in Asia have drunk for thousands of years, is better for us than many other hot drinks. While coffee has 135 milligrams of caffeine and black tea has 50 milligrams, a cup of green tea has only 30 milligrams of caffeine. In addition, green tea might help fight several serious health problems. Some scientists say that green tea might lower the risk of cancer. Green tea may also help keep teeth healthy and strong. In addition, it might help people lose weight and may protect us against some heart problems. On top of these benefits, green tea tastes delicious.

1. What is the article about?
2. How much caffeine is in green tea?
3. Which has less caffeine, green tea or coffee?
4. Can green tea help prevent colds?
5. Can green tea help prevent cancer?

EXERCISE 13 Clustering

What are the main idea, points, and subpoints of the reading? Cluster the ideas in the reading. Write your cluster in your notebook. Follow the example on page 56.

Your Portfolio

Review the list of changes you wrote in Bridging to the Future on page 60. Then put the list in your portfolio.

Summing Up

I can:

- ☐ **1.** Read about caffeine.
- ☐ **2.** Read about getting enough rest.
- ☐ **3.** Distinguish between main idea, points, and subpoints.
- ☐ **4.** Understand the prefix **over-**.
- ☐ **5.** Use clustering.
- ☐ **6.** ______________________________

Tools and Technology

In this unit, you will:

1. Read about Thomas Edison.
2. Read about the invention of the lightbulb.
3. Decide when to skip unknown vocabulary.
4. Understand the verb **could.**
5. Use a time line.

Accessing Information

Talk About It

Look at the inventions. What are they? How did they change people's lives?

You Decide

Why do people invent things?

Key Vocabulary

A. In this unit, you will read about inventions such as movies and the electric lightbulb. First, work with a partner. In your notebook, write a list of words you know about lightbulbs.

B. Study the vocabulary.

develop–work on something over time until it's ready
invent–make a completely new product
inventor–someone who makes a completely new product
invention–completely new product
stick to–keep doing something until it's finished
improve–make something better
electricity–it makes lightbulbs, TVs, and other things work
electric–related to electricity

EXERCISE 1 Vocabulary

Write the word from Key Vocabulary, part B on the line.

1. Thomas Edison was a famous ____________________.
2. He ____________________ many important things, such as record players.
3. Edison's first record players weren't very good, but he worked hard to ____________________ them.
4. Many of Edison's inventions needed electricity, so he started an ____________________ company.
5. Edison worked hard–up to 12 hours a day. He said that if you work hard and ____________________ your goals, you will succeed.

EXERCISE 2 Before You Read

A. When we read, we can use the context (the other words around the word) to figure out the meaning. Read the sentences. Use the context to figure out the meanings of the underlined words.

> Thomas Edison started a (1) <u>profitable</u> company and became rich. Edison used his (2) <u>wealth</u> to develop more inventions.

B. If we can't figure out the *exact* meaning of new words, we can look them up in a dictionary. However, sometimes we may understand the main idea of the reading without understanding the exact meaning of some of the words. Then we don't need to look up those words in a dictionary.

As you read the encyclopedia article on page 64, pay attention to the word **rubber.** Do you need to understand the word's exact meaning to understand the main idea of the reading? Why? Write a few words in your notebook.

What would your life be like without movies, electric lights, or recorded music?

CD 2 TRACK 1

Edison, Thomas Alva 1847–1931

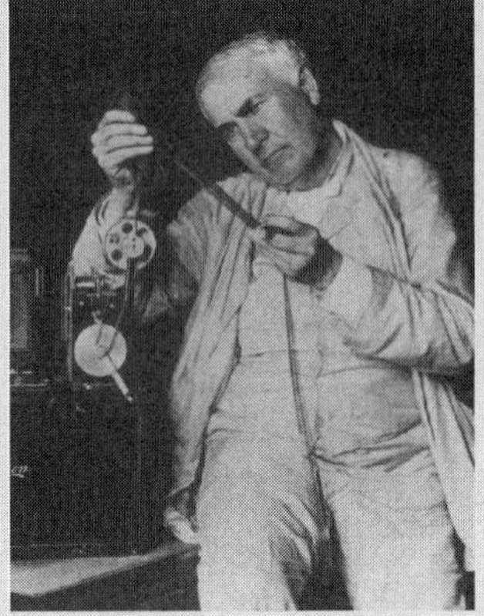

Movies, electric lights, and recorded music completely changed the way we live. One person we should thank for these inventions is Thomas Edison. But who was Thomas Edison?

Thomas Edison was born in Ohio in 1847. As a child, he was interested in how things worked. He was always asking adults to explain how machines worked. If they couldn't explain, he got upset! When he got a little older, he liked to read books by famous scientists. As a teenager, he started a small newspaper, which he sold to people on trains. He was the first person in the U.S. to do this, and he made a lot of money.

Edison's first real job was with a telegraph company. (The telegraph was an early system to send messages across long distances.) He helped the telegraph company invent better systems, and his inventions were very successful. He became wealthy, and in 1875 he quit his job so he could invent full time. After that, Edison invented thousands of things. His most famous inventions were the electric lightbulb, records and record players, and movies.

Edison developed the first lightbulb that people could use. Edison tried thousands of different ideas. Finally, he developed a lightbulb that was inexpensive and could last a long time. However, people couldn't use the lightbulb without electricity, so Edison started the country's first electric company, in New York City. Soon cities all over the country had electric companies.

Edison also worked on developing records and record players. He tried many different materials for records, including metal and rubber. Finally, in 1887 he figured out a way to make records out of a metal called tin. The records sounded good and were easy to make. Edison continued to improve his invention. Soon people all over the world were listening to Edison's records on his record players.

Edison developed ways to make and show movies. Edison's first movie was only a few seconds long—it showed him sneezing! At first, people had to look in a small box to see movies. Later, Edison's company figured out a way to show movies in theaters. Edison also made one of the first hit movies, *The Great Train Robbery.*

Edison was very intelligent, but he also worked hard. Sometimes he worked 12 hours a day or more. He also worked for years on many of his inventions. Edison said, "The three things that are most essential to achievement are common sense, hard work, and stick-to-it-tive-ness." Edison's life shows that if we stick to our goals, we can succeed.

Edison's Achievements

Records and Record Players 1887

Movies 1894

EXERCISE 3 After You Read

A. Review your answer to Exercise 2, part B on page 63. Do you need to understand the exact meaning of **rubber** in order to understand the article? Talk over your ideas with a partner. Share your ideas with the class.

B. The reading contains the word **stick-to-it-tive-ness.** This isn't a real word. Edison invented it. What did Edison mean? You already know what **stick to** means. Use the word **stick to** and other clues to figure out the meaning of **stick-to-it-tive-ness.**

EXERCISE 4 Answer the Questions

Write the answers in your notebook.

1. When was Edison born?
2. What did Edison do as a child?
3. What was Edison's first real job?
4. Why did he quit that job?
5. What were Edison's most famous inventions?
6. Why did Edison start an electric company?
7. Did people like Edison's record player? How do you know?
8. Did Edison stick to his goals? Why do you think so?

Teamwork

Work with a partner. Student A looks at the information on Edison's achievements on page 64. Student B looks at the information on Edison's achievements on page 124. Complete the chart. Ask your partner questions.

Achievement	Year
Lightbulb	
Records and Record Players	
Movies	
The Great Train Robbery	

EXERCISE 5 Time Line

A. A time line is a good way to organize information about the past. Look at the time line of Edison's life. Add the year Edison invented the lightbulb to the time line. Write **lightbulb** over the time line.

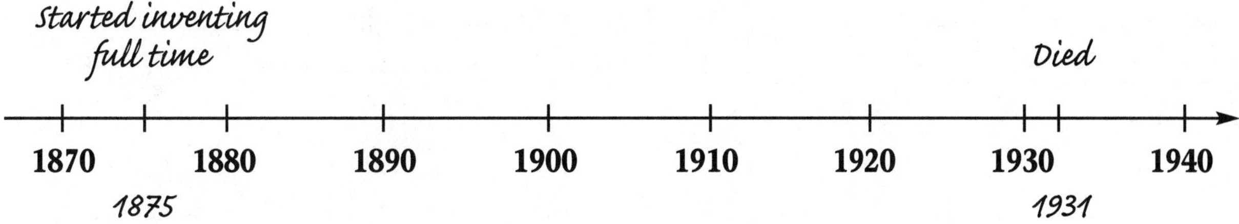

B. Use the information from Teamwork to complete the time line.

Giving Voice

Talk It Over

A. Work with a partner. Describe Edison's character in a few words or phrases. Share your sentences with the class.

B. Edison was successful because he stuck to his goals. Why don't people stick to their goals? Write a list. Share it with the class.

EXERCISE 6 Your Goals

A. What are some of your goals? How will you achieve them? For example, you probably have the goal of learning English. You will achieve your goal by coming to class regularly. Complete the chart.

Goals	How I'll Achieve My Goals

B. Share your completed chart with the class. Then use it to keep track of your progress. Check your chart regularly to make sure that you are sticking to your goals.

LANGUAGE NOTE
The Verb *Could*

The reading on Edison uses the verb **could. Could** is the past form of **can.** Understanding **could** will help you when you read. Study the examples.

People **could** use Edison's lightbulb because it was inexpensive and lasted a long time.

People **couldn't** use his lightbulbs if their homes didn't have electricity.

Review the reading on page 64. Circle the examples of **could.**

EXERCISE 7 Could or Couldn't

Write **could** or **couldn't** on the line.

1. Edison __________ work full time and work on his inventions, too, so he quit his job.
2. At first, inventors __________ develop lightbulbs that lasted a long time.
3. Edison thought that he __________ develop a good electric lightbulb.
4. Edison thought that he __________ succeed if he worked long hours in his lab on the project.
5. Finally, Edison developed an inexpensive lightbulb that __________ last a long time.

Accessing Information

Edison's Failures

Edison's lab

Most people remember Edison for his successes, such as the lightbulb and the record player. But Edison's ideas weren't always successful. For example, cement fascinated Edison. He figured out ways to make it stronger and less expensive. But he also thought that many things could be built from it. He developed a way to build houses with only cement. The houses were inexpensive, but no one wanted to live in them. He also wanted to build record players from cement. He thought that the record players would be strong and last a long time. But the cement record players were too heavy!

Edison also wanted to find a better way to get iron, silver, and other metals from the ground. He spent millions of dollars on this invention, but it never worked. Finally, he gave up.

Edison worked long and hard on all of his inventions, and many were successful, but these two were not. Even after these failures, he continued to invent other successful products. Edison showed that if we don't succeed on one project, we can still be successful on others.

Talk About It

Which of Edison's inventions weren't successful? Why? What did Edison do?

You Decide

When someone isn't successful at something, what should the person do? Why?

STUDY SKILL
Using a Notebook

Thomas Edison used notebooks to help him. He wrote down new ideas and drew pictures of his inventions.

You can use a notebook, too. You probably take notes in class already. You can also take notes on readings. You can write down new ideas. Or you can use your notebook for a journal. How do you want to use your notebook in the future? Write a few ideas in your notebook.

READING STRATEGY
Decide When to Skip Unknown Vocabulary

When we read, we often find words we don't know. When this happens, we can use the context to figure out the meaning. Or we can also use a dictionary to look up the meaning of the word. But sometimes we can understand the reading without knowing the exact meaning of the word. For example, look at this sentence from the reading on page 67:

> Edison also wanted to find a better way to get iron, silver, and other metals from the ground.

From the context, you can figure out that **iron** is probably a metal. But you don't know the *exact* meaning. However, you don't need to know the exact meaning of iron to understand the most important ideas of the reading: Some of Edison's inventions didn't work, and one of them was a new way to get metals from the ground. So when you don't need to know the exact meaning of a word, skip it and continue reading.

EXERCISE 8 Skipping Unknown Vocabulary

A. Read the paragraph. Do you need to know the exact meanings of the underlined words in order to understand the sentences? Why or why not? Write a few words on the lines.

> Thomas Edison wasn't the only important inventor of his time. At about the same time Edison was working, Alexander Graham Bell invented the telephone. Like Edison, Bell was a hard worker. Reportedly, the first words that were transmitted over the telephone were said by Bell to his assistant. After Bell injured himself, Bell said, "Mr. Watson–come here–I want to see you." When the assistant came to help Bell, Bell knew his invention was a success.

1. Reportedly: ______________________________
2. transmitted: ______________________________

B. Work with a partner. Talk over your answers to part A. Be ready to explain each answer to the class.

EXERCISE 9 Before You Read

As you read the article on pages 69 and 70, decide whether you need to know the exact meaning of the word **carbon.**

How was the lightbulb invented?

CD 2 TRACK 2

THE STORY OF THE LIGHTBULB

Thomas Edison is known because of his countless inventions. His inventions improved the lives of many people, and we still use many of his inventions today. Many people thank Edison for the invention of the light bulb, but Edison did not actually invent the lightbulb himself. He only improved on the ideas of many other inventors. After Edison, other inventors continued to improve the lightbulb until we got the lightbulb of today. How did they develop the lightbulb? First, let's look at how lightbulbs work.

All lightbulbs work the same way: Electricity enters the bulb through metal contacts at the bottom of the bulb. Inside the bulb, the electricity passes through wires and reaches a filament—a very thin piece of material. The electricity makes the filament become white-hot and give off light. However, no one could find a filament that was inexpensive and would last a long time.

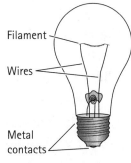

Filament

Wires

Metal contacts

In 1820, an inventor from England named Warren de la Rue developed one of the earliest lightbulbs. Its filament was made of platinum—a very expensive metal. The platinum filament could last a long time. However, the platinum made the lightbulbs too expensive.

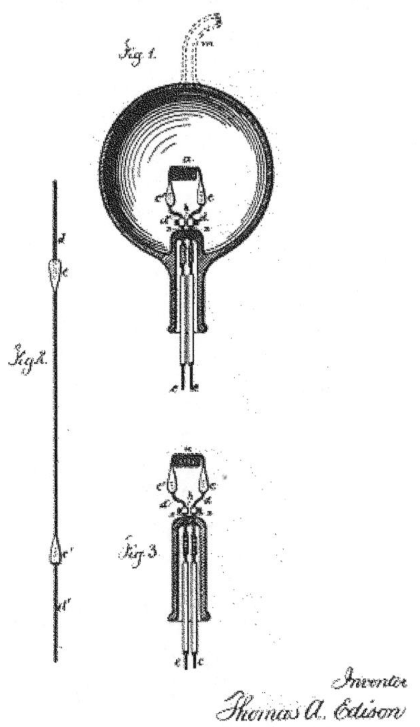

Edison's drawing for his lightbulb

Edison and inventor Joseph Wilson Swan, who was working in England, both invented the carbon filament at about the same time, in 1879. Carbon was inexpensive and could last a long time. By 1880, Edison invented a lightbulb that would last for 1,200 hours. In order to keep the carbon from burning, Edison had to remove all the air from the inside of the lightbulb. These lightbulbs were inexpensive, but they were not very bright. People began to use Edison's new lightbulbs, but inventors continued to look for better materials for filaments.

continued 

Finally, in about 1910, an inventor named William Coolidge used a metal named tungsten in lightbulbs. Tungsten was inexpensive and could make very bright light, but it couldn't last for a long time.

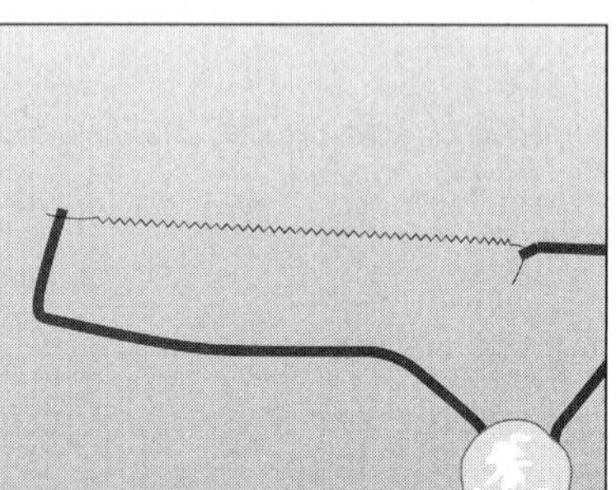

Coolidge kept testing tungsten. He put the tungsten in a coil. Then it could last longer. Soon everyone was using his lightbulbs. We still use tungsten lightbulbs today.

Today, we have many different kinds of lightbulbs to choose from. There are colored lightbulbs and lightbulbs especially for reading. There are special lightbulbs for headlights, ovens, and theaters. In addition, inventors have developed new kinds of lights, such as neon. But people everywhere should thank Edison for developing the first lightbulb that everyone could use.

EXERCISE 10 After You Read

Review your answer to Exercise 9 on page 68. Do you need to know the exact meaning of **carbon** to understand the reading? Or can you skip this word? Why do you think so? Share your answer with the class.

EXERCISE 11 Answer the Questions

Write the answers in your notebook.

1. Did Edison invent the lightbulb alone?
2. What is a filament?
3. What happens when electricity passes through the filament?
4. What was the problem with Warren de la Rue's lightbulb?
5. Who invented the carbon filament?
6. What was good about the carbon filament? What was the problem with it?
7. Who found a better material for filaments? What was the material?
8. Why did Coolidge put the tungsten in a coil?

EXERCISE 12 How Lightbulbs Work

A. Number the steps in order from 1 to 4.

_______ **a.** The filament becomes white-hot, which makes light.

_______ **b.** The electricity passes through wires.

_______ **c.** The electricity reaches the filament.

_______ **d.** Electricity enters the lightbulb through metal contacts at the bottom of the bulb.

B. Work with a partner. Take turns explaining how a lightbulb works. Use the drawing.

EXERCISE 13 Time Line

A. When were the different filaments invented? Use the information in the reading on pages 69 and 70 to complete the chart.

Filament	Year
platinum	

B. Add the information in the chart to the time line.

Reading Journal

Complete a copy of the reading journal form on page 126. Keep the form in your notebook or portfolio.

Taking Action

A. By the time of Edison's death in 1931, most cities and towns in the U.S. had electric lights and street lights. Before then, people used gas lights and candles. How did electricity help communities? Talk over your ideas with your partner. Share your partner's ideas with the class.

B. What other inventions have helped communities? Work with a partner. Think of one or two other inventions. Tell how they helped communities. Write your ideas in your notebook. Share your ideas with the class.

Bridging to the Future

What are some inventions that we need today? Work with a partner. Write a few ideas in your notebooks. What do you want to invent? Write that down, too.

Family Connection

How can you save money on electricity at home? Work with a partner and make a list. Share your list with the class.

Enriching Your Vocabulary

Look at the lightbulb package. What do the words mean?

light output–the amount of light the bulb produces. The higher the number, the brighter the light.

energy used–the amount of electricity the bulb uses. The higher the number, the more electricity it uses. Usually, lamps have labels that say the maximum number of watts a lightbulb can have. Never use a bulb with too many watts. It could start a fire.

life–the number of hours the lightbulb will last

What are some other words we use to talk about lightbulbs? Work with a small group and make a list. Share your list with the class.

Review

EXERCISE 14 Answer the Questions

A. Read the article. Write the answers in your notebook.

Who Invented the Windshield Wiper?

Windshield wipers are a part of every car. They help drivers see the road when it's raining or snowing. We owe the windshield wiper to two women inventors, Mary Anderson and Charlotte Bridgwood. In about 1900, Mary Anderson noticed that streetcar drivers couldn't see very well when it was raining, snowing, or sleeting. Her system let drivers clean their windows from inside the car. The wipers weren't automatic, but they kept the windows clear. Car companies began to use the invention, too. By 1916, all new cars had her windshield wipers. A year later, in 1917, Charlotte Bridgwood invented electric windshield wipers. The next time you're in a car and it's raining, remember that these two inventions are keeping you safe.

1. Who invented the first windshield wipers?
2. Were the first windshield wipers automatic?
3. Who invented automatic windshield wipers?
4. Were windshield wipers a success? How do you know?

B. Find the word **sleeting** in the article. Do you need to know its exact meaning to understand the article? Why or why not? Write a few words on the line.

____

Your Portfolio

Review the list of ways to save money on electricity you wrote in Family Connection on page 72. Put a copy of your list in your notebook.

Summing Up

I can:

- ☐ **1.** Read about Thomas Edison.
- ☐ **2.** Read about the invention of the lightbulb.
- ☐ **3.** Decide when to skip unknown vocabulary.
- ☐ **4.** Understand the verb **could**.
- ☐ **5.** Use a time line.
- ☐ **6.** ______________________________

Our History

In this unit, you will:

1. Read about immigration to the U.S.
2. Read about a multicultural celebration.
3. Check your comprehension while reading.
4. Understand sentences with **before** and **after.**
5. Understand a family tree.

Accessing Information

Talk About It

Where are the people? What are they doing? What are they thinking and feeling?

You Decide

Why do immigrants come to the U.S.? Did your family immigrate? Why?

Key Vocabulary

A. In this unit, you will read about immigration. First you will read about the history of immigration to the U.S. Then you will read about a festival in Texas that celebrates immigrants' heritage. First, work with a partner. In your notebook, write a list of words you know about immigration.

B. Study the vocabulary.

immigrant–someone who moves to a new country

related to–part of the same family

celebration–party or time of fun together for a special reason

celebrate–have a celebration

population–the people who live in a place

ethnic group–group of people who have the same race, nationality, religion, and/or culture

EXERCISE 1 Vocabulary

Write the word from Key Vocabulary, part B on the line.

1. We ____________________ New Year's Day on January 1.
2. Juan Villa is an ____________________ from Mexico. He came to the U.S. in 1992.
3. New York has a ____________________ of about 8 million people.
4. Of course I am ____________________ Laura. She's my sister!

EXERCISE 2 Before You Read

As you read, it's a good idea to stop and ask yourself questions. If you can answer the questions, you can continue reading. If you can't answer the question, reread to find the answer. Read the first paragraph of the article on page 76. Then read question 1. Write the answer in your notebook. Continue with the other questions.

1. After paragraph 1: How did immigration change from 1776 to the late 1880s?
2. After paragraph 2: Why is Ellis Island important?
3. After paragraph 3: What happened at Ellis Island?
4. After paragraph 4: Why did Ellis Island close?
5. After paragraph 5: What is Ellis Island today?

What is Ellis Island?

CD 2 TRACK 3

Ellis Island: A Symbol of U.S. Immigration

In many ways, the history of the U.S. is the history of immigration. Except for Native Americans, everyone who lives in the U.S. comes from immigrants. After the U.S. became independent in 1776, large numbers of people began to immigrate. By the late 1880s, the number of immigrants was increasing dramatically. During this time of high immigration, one place was associated with immigration to the U.S.: Ellis Island.

Ellis Island is an island near New York City. From 1892 to 1954, Ellis Island was an immigration station for immigrants arriving on the East Coast. These immigrants came mostly from Europe. Over 12 million immigrants entered the U.S. through Ellis Island. On its busiest days, 10,000 people would go through Ellis Island. Today, over 100 million people in the U.S. are related to people who entered the U.S. through Ellis Island. That's about 40% of the U.S. population.

Immigrants usually reached Ellis Island after a long trip at sea. They often traveled in crowded ships, and sometimes trips took several weeks. After immigrants arrived, they went to Ellis Island on special boats. Before immigrants could enter the U.S., they had to pass medical and legal examinations. Immigrants would often stay at Ellis Island for several days, so the immigration station had hundreds of beds and a restaurant. After the immigrants entered the U.S., they could use a special ticket office on Ellis Island to buy train tickets to other parts of the U.S.

Ellis Island became less busy in the 1950s. Fewer and fewer immigrants were coming from Europe, and more and more immigrants were coming from Asia, Latin America, and Africa to the West Coast and other parts of the U.S. Many immigrants also began arriving by air. As a result, the immigration station at Ellis Island was no longer needed. After the station closed in 1954, the buildings fell into disrepair. After the buildings were repaired, Ellis Island reopened as a museum in 1992.

Today, visitors to the museum can learn about immigration. They can see the places where immigrants arrived, slept, filled out forms, and waited. Exhibits show the hard life that immigrants faced in the U.S. Other exhibits show the history of immigration to the U.S. from all parts of the world. Ellis Island also has an oral history project. This project has interviewed more than 1,500 immigrants who passed through Ellis Island. The stories were used to create a play about immigration that visitors can see while on the island.

Even though Ellis Island is now a museum, more immigrants than ever are coming to the U.S. At present, about 11% of the people in the U.S. are immigrants. Immigration is truly one of the most important parts of U.S. history.

Sally and Pilar Mendez immigrated to the U.S. from Spain in 1923. They were 14 and 20. They were interviewed for the Ellis Island Oral History Project. They said that the best part of coming to the U.S. was the ability to go to school. At that time, many girls in Spain did not complete their educations. Both Sally and Pilar were able to go to school, and the family was able to educate all their children. Sally said, "I sent the kids to school, to college and everything. Over there we couldn't."

EXERCISE 3 After You Read

Review your answers to Exercise 2 on page 75. Were your answers correct? Did answering the questions as you read help you understand the article better? Discuss your ideas with a partner. Share your ideas with the class.

EXERCISE 4 Answer the Questions

Write the answers in your notebook.

1. Where is Ellis Island?
2. Why is the immigration station at Ellis Island important?
3. How did immigration change in the 1950s?
4. What can people do at Ellis Island today?
5. Who are Sally and Pilar?
6. What was important about coming to the U.S. for Sally and Pilar?

Teamwork

A. Look at the article again. Write a **wh-** question (who, what, when, where, why, how) about each of the paragraphs.

1. ______________________________
2. ______________________________
3. ______________________________
4. ______________________________
5. ______________________________
6. ______________________________

B. Work with a partner. Student A asks Student B the questions on this page. Student B writes the answers on page 124. Student A checks Student B's answers. Then switch roles and repeat part B.

Enriching Your Vocabulary

We use many words to talk about immigration. Study the vocabulary.

visa–permission from a country to enter its country
citizen–legal member of a country, state, etc.
naturalization–becoming a U.S. citizen
permanent resident–immigrant who has permission to live in the U.S. but is not a citizen
green card–U.S. government document for permanent residents
immigration status–type of permission an immigrant has to stay in the U.S.

Giving Voice

Talk It Over

What's your family history? Where is your family from? Do you have a lot of relatives? Where do your relatives live now? Do you have relatives in other countries? Talk over your ideas with a partner. Share your partner's ideas with the class.

EXERCISE 5 Your Family Tree

A. A family tree shows information about a family and its history. Study the family tree of the Feng family. Is the family large or small? How many people are in it?

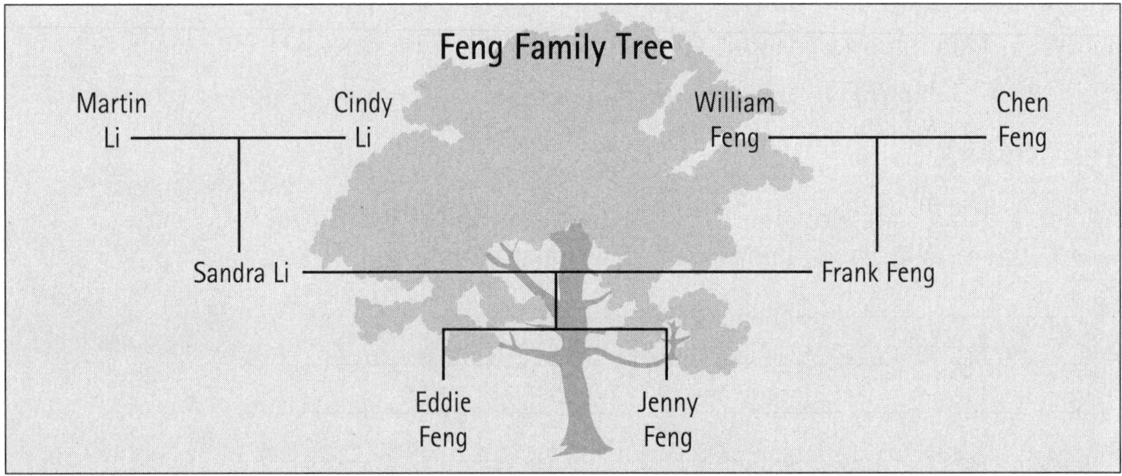

B. Complete the chart with information about your family. Write the names of your relatives in the boxes. You may also write about another family or about a famous family you know about.

Relatives	Names
You and your brothers and sisters	
Your parents	
Your aunts and uncles	
Your cousins	
Your grandparents	

C. Use the information in part B to draw a family tree. Use the family tree in part A as a model. Share your family tree with a small group.

Accessing Information

Angel Island

Angel Island was an immigration station similar to Ellis Island. Located near San Francisco, Angel Island was the location of an immigration station from 1910 to 1940 for immigrants who entered the U.S. on the West Coast. Immigrants from China, Japan, Russia, Mexico, and Australia used the immigration station.

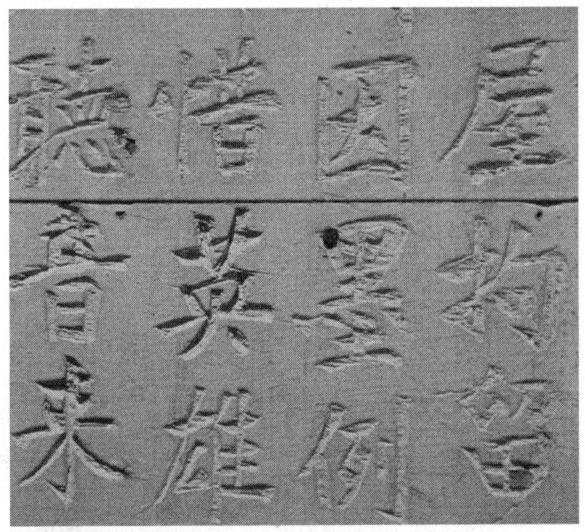

Poetry from the walls of Angel Island

The experience of immigrants who used Angel Island was different from the experience of European immigrants who entered the U.S. through Ellis Island. There was a lot of discrimination against immigrants from Asia, and immigrants from Asia had to wait a long time before they could enter the U.S. They had to pass difficult interviews. While immigrants were waiting to enter the U.S., they wrote poetry on the walls of the buildings.

In 1970, the government was going to close Angel Island. But a government worker saw the poetry in the buildings. He helped save the buildings on Angel Island. Like Ellis Island, Angel Island is now a museum about U.S. immigration. Visitors can see the old immigration station and see exhibits about the lives of immigrants from Asia. Visitors can still see the poetry that immigrants wrote on the walls of the buildings.

Talk About It
What is Angel Island? Why is it important? Why did immigrants at Angel Island have a different experience than immigrants at Ellis Island?

You Decide
What is difficult about being an immigrant? Why do people immigrate? Is immigration easier or harder now than in the past?

READING STRATEGY
Check Your Comprehension While Reading

When you read, it's a good idea to check from time to time to make sure that you understand the article. After each paragraph, you should ask yourself a question that begins with one of the **wh-** question words. If you can't answer the question, you should go back and reread the paragraph. For example, ask yourself this question about the first paragraph of the reading on Angel Island on page 79:

What was Angel Island?

If you can't answer the question, go back and read the paragraph again.

EXERCISE 6 Checking Your Comprehension

Read the article. After you read each paragraph, write a question on the line. Then answer the question.

Angel Island is a museum today because of the work of four people: Alexander Weiss, George Araki, Mak Takahashi, and Paul Chow. Alexander Weiss is the park worker who saw the poetry in 1970. He called George Araki, who was a professor at a university in the area. Professor Araki and a photographer named Mak Takahashi took pictures of the buildings and the poetry on the walls. They showed the photographs to a community group in San Francisco, the Bay Area Asian Americans.

Question:____

Answer:____

The Bay Area Asian Americans began to work to save the old immigration station. A leader of that organization, Paul Chow, started a new group to save the immigration station. Finally, in 1976, the state of California agreed to save the immigration station. Because of the work of these groups and individuals, we visitors can see the immigration station today.

Question:____

Answer:____

EXERCISE 7 Before You Read

As you read the article on pages 81 and 82, stop reading after each paragraph. Write a question in your notebook about the paragraph. Then write the answer to the question. If you can't answer the question correctly, reread the paragraph to find the answer. Then write the answer. There are seven paragraphs (the last one is short). You should have six questions and six answers for the first six paragraphs.

What U.S. city has a two-week festival to celebrate its history and traditions?

CD 2 TRACK 4

Fiesta Celebrates San Antonio's Past

San Antonio, Texas, has a fascinating mixture of immigrants from all over the world, including Europe, Mexico, Central and South America, Africa, and Asia. A good time to learn about San Antonio's past is during Fiesta. Fiesta is a very old event. It began over 100 years ago as a week-long celebration all over the city. Since then, Fiesta has grown to over 200 events during two weeks in April. Fiesta includes parades, concerts, parties, dances, contests, and special events. Events celebrate all of the different ethnic groups that have contributed to the history of San Antonio. What is the ethnic history of San Antonio, and how is it reflected in Fiesta?

Immigration to San Antonio is very similar to immigration in the rest of the U.S. Before Europeans came to San Antonio, Native Americans lived in the area. Spanish settlers began coming in the 17th century. After the Spanish settlers arrived, they built churches and other buildings. Some of these buildings still stand today. Settlers from Spain and Mexico continued to come to the area. However, like the rest of the U.S. during the 19th century, San Antonio began to receive immigrants from northern and western Europe. Later, U.S. immigration began to include people from Africa, Asia, and Latin America. San Antonio began to receive immigrants from these places, too. Today, San Antonio has an especially large Mexican population because Mexico is so close by.

During Fiesta, visitors can see events and activities that reflect all of these groups. Museums often have special events that explore the area's Native American past. The museums show old objects from Native Americans in the area, including clothes, beautiful dishes, and other objects. At special exhibits in parks, visitors can see Native American crafts and meet descendents of Native Americans.

continued →

During Fiesta, visitors can find out about German contributions to San Antonio at the King William Fair. The King William Fair takes place in the King William neighborhood of San Antonio. This neighborhood was named for the king of Germany during the time many immigrants moved to Texas. Many German immigrants became wealthy, and they built beautiful homes in this neighborhood. During the fair, visitors can see the neighborhood, tour some of the homes, and see beautiful gardens and parks. Fiesta also has special concerts with German music and food.

Visitors can see the Mexican contribution to San Antonio very clearly in the many parades and concerts that take place during Fiesta. One of the most famous parades takes place on the river that runs through the middle of downtown San Antonio. Many large and small boats take part in the parade, and each of them has beautiful decorations. Many famous performers of Mexican music, including singers and bands, participate in the parades.

Immigrants from other countries participate in Fiesta in different ways. A few years ago, a Chinese group had a dragon in one of the parades. Vietnamese organizations often participate in the parades, too. Most years, African-American groups organize jazz concerts. And people can hear music and try food from countries such as France, Greece, Mexico, Spain, and Ireland at different times and places throughout Fiesta. One year, a children's choir from Ghana gave concerts and participated in the parade.

Fiesta is a great way for families to learn more about the multicultural past of San Antonio.

EXERCISE 8 After You Read

A. Work with a partner. Review the questions and answers you wrote in your notebook for Exercise 7 on page 80. Check your partner's work. Did your partner answer his or her questions correctly? Are all your answers correct? If necessary, reread the article on pages 81 and 82.

B. How did asking questions as you read help you read? Why? Talk over your ideas with your partner. Share your partner's ideas with the class.

LANGUAGE NOTE
Sentences with *Before and After*

We use **before** and **after** to tell what happened first and second.

Before Europeans came to San Antonio, Native Americans lived in the area.

After the Spanish settlers arrived, they built churches and other buildings.

Review the article on pages 81 and 82. Underline the sentences with **before** and **after.**

EXERCISE 9 Answer the Questions

Write the answers in your notebook.

1. What is Fiesta?
2. When does it take place?
3. Is it an old event? How old?
4. What different ethnic groups came to San Antonio?
5. What Native American things can you see at Fiesta?
6. What can visitors see at the King William Fair?
7. What is unusual about one of the parades?
8. What other ethnic groups besides Mexicans participate in Fiesta?

EXERCISE 10 People in San Antonio

When did people first come to San Antonio? Number the groups in order from 1 to 4.

_________ **a.** immigrants from Europe

_________ **b.** Spanish settlers and immigrants from Mexico

_________ **c.** Native Americans

_________ **d.** immigrants from Asia and Africa

EXERCISE 11 Visiting Fiesta

Work with a partner. What would you do at Fiesta? What culture would you learn about? Complete the chart.

Event	Culture
King William Fair	Germany

Reading Journal

Complete a copy of the reading journal form on page 126. Keep the form in your notebook or portfolio.

Taking Action

A. Your class is going to participate in a celebration similar to Fiesta in your city. What ethnic groups are in your class? How do you want to show each group's contributions? Work as a class. Create a class plan for how you will participate in the celebration.

B. Review your plan as a class. Organize part of your plan as a special class event. You might have a food fair, a craft fair, or special exhibits about the ethnic groups in your class. After you organize the event, invite another class to participate.

Bridging to the Future

A. What parts of your culture are you proud of? For example, you might be proud that your country has traveled in space. Or you might be proud of famous inventors and inventions. Write a list of things you are proud of. Share your list with the class.

B. Work with a partner. Why is feeling proud of your culture important? How will this pride help you in school? At work? In the community? Share your ideas with the class.

Workplace Connection

Companies have histories, too. Work with a partner. Investigate the history of your company or an important company in your area. Who started it? When? Who owns it now? What was the company like when it started? How has it changed? Use the Internet and people at the company to help you. Use the information to write a few sentences about the history of the company in your notebook.

STUDY SKILL
Using Parts of a Textbook

The reading about Ellis Island on page 76 is similar to the information we find in many textbooks. You are reading a textbook right now. We also use textbooks in most other classes. Textbooks usually have similar parts:

contents—a list that shows the organization of the book

glossary—a list of important vocabulary and definitions

index—a list of the information in the book and the pages the information is on

Look at another textbook. Write a list of the parts in your notebook. Tell what each part is for. Share the book and the list with the class.

Review

EXERCISE 12 Monitoring Comprehension
Read the article. After you read each paragraph, write a question and an answer on the lines.

More and more people are researching their family histories and creating family trees. Roberta Gonzalez researched her family tree, and the results were fascinating. In her mother's family, she found out that her great-grandparents had immigrated to Mexico from Germany. They left Germany to get religious freedom. Later, the family moved to Texas to find work.

Question:____________________________________

Answer:____________________________________

On her father's side, her great-grandfather immigrated from Spain to Cuba. In 1932, the family moved to the U.S. Roberta said, "I found out that my family was rich in Cuba but lost everything because of economic problems. So they moved to the U.S. First they went to Miami, but later we moved to Texas." In Texas, she met her future husband, Bob Gonzalez.

Question:____________________________________

Answer:____________________________________

Your Portfolio

Review the list you wrote in Bridging to the Future, part A on page 84. Put a copy of the list in your portfolio.

Summing Up

I can:

- ☐ **1.** Read about immigration to the U.S.
- ☐ **2.** Read about a multicultural celebration.
- ☐ **3.** Check my comprehension while reading.
- ☐ **4.** Understand sentences with **before** and **after.**
- ☐ **5.** Understand a family tree.
- ☐ **6.** ____________________________________

Home Sweet Home

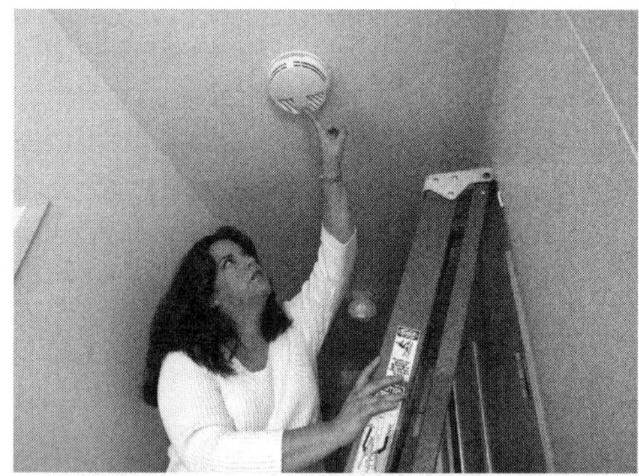

In this unit, you will:

1. Read about smoke detectors.
2. Read about what to do in case of a tornado.
3. Skim for the main idea.
4. Understand simple conditions with **if.**
5. Use a diagram to organize information.

Accessing Information

Talk About It

Look at the pictures. What's happening? What are the people doing?

You Decide

How do you keep your home safe? How do you stay safe in bad weather?

Key Vocabulary

A. In this unit, you will read about keeping safe. First, you will read about ways to make your family safer from fire. Then, you will read about a very dangerous kind of storm, a tornado. First, work with a partner. In your notebook, write a list of different kinds of dangers, such as a fire.

B. Study the vocabulary.

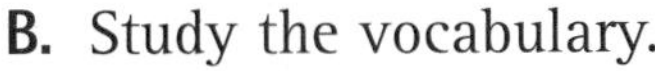

fire 

battery 

flashlight 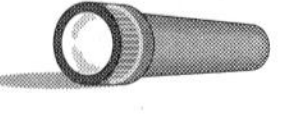

lightning

thunderstorm—bad storm with thunder and lightning
hail—balls of ice that fall from the sky
smoke detector—machine that makes noise if there is smoke in the house
tornado—very dangerous storm with very strong winds
destroy—damage something badly so it can't be used again

EXERCISE 1 Vocabulary

Write the word from Key Vocabulary, part B on the line.

1. The lights aren't working. Do we have a ______________?
2. The radio isn't working. It needs a new ______________.
3. A ______________ will keep your family safe if there is a fire.
4. I couldn't sleep last night. The noise from the ______________ kept me awake.
5. My neighbor has to buy a new car. Last night, a fire completely ______________ his car.

EXERCISE 2 Before You Read

A. When you skim, you read quickly to find out the main idea. Then, after you know the main idea, you reread more carefully to find out the details. Work with a partner. Skim the article on page 88. Write the main idea of the article in your notebook. Then think about your background knowledge about this topic. (Background knowledge is information you already know about a topic.) Write a few notes in your notebook.

B. Now reread the article more carefully. Use your background knowledge to help you understand the details of the reading.

How can you keep your home safe 24 hours a day?

CD 2 TRACK 5

Smoke Detectors Save Lives

A simple device can make anyone's home safer.

According to experts, over 2,200 people die in the U.S. each year from fires in their homes. About 1,100 of these people are children. Many of these fires happen at night when people are asleep. Most of these people die because they do not have working smoke detectors. A smoke detector makes a loud noise when there is a fire. That way, people can get out of the house in time.

A home should have at least one smoke detector on each floor. Don't put it near the kitchen. The best place to put a smoke detector is near the bedrooms. If the bedrooms are far apart, put a smoke detector near each bedroom. If anyone has hearing problems, get a special smoke detector that makes a bright light.

You should test your smoke detector once a month. Follow the instructions. Usually, you test a smoke detector by pressing a button on the detector. If the alarm sounds, the smoke detector is working. On other detectors, you look for a small light or you shine a flashlight on the detector. You should change the battery in your smoke detectors twice a year. A good time to change the battery is when you change your clocks in the spring and fall for daylight saving time. After you change the battery, test the detector to make sure it works. You should replace a smoke detector when it's ten years old. If you don't know the age of your smoke detector, you should get a new one.

A fire can move very quickly. So if your smoke detector goes off, it's important to get outside as soon as you know there is a fire. For this reason, everyone should know what to do in a fire, especially children. Tell children that in a fire they should go outside right away and then call 9-1-1. Don't stop to get things. Just make sure that everyone gets outside as quickly as possible.

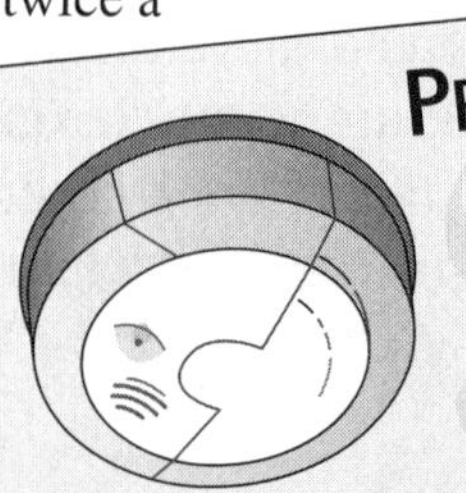

PREMIUM SMOKE DETECTOR

Features:

Uses a 9-volt battery
Use a flashlight to test
Ten-year guarantee

$14.99

EXERCISE 3 After You Read

Review your answer to Exercise 2, part A on page 87. Was your answer correct? Did your background knowledge help you when you read the article? Talk over your ideas with your partner. Share your ideas with the class.

EXERCISE 4 Answer the Questions

A. Write the answers in your notebook.

1. How many people die in home fires each year in the U.S.?
2. What is a smoke detector?
3. How often should you check a smoke detector?
4. How often should you change the battery?
5. What should you do in case of a fire?

B. Look at the diagram in the article. Where do you put a smoke detector? Do you put a smoke detector in a high place or a low place? In the living room or the hall? Write a few words in your notebook. Then think about your answer. What information was in the diagram? What information was in the reading? How did the diagram help you? Write a few words in your notebook.

Teamwork

A. Work with a partner. Student A looks at the information on the Premium Smoke Detector on page 88. Student B looks at the information on the Basic Smoke Detector on page 124. Complete the chart. Ask your partner questions.

	Premium Smoke Detector	Basic Smoke Detector
How do you test it?		
How much does it cost?		
How long is the guarantee?		

B. Work with a partner. Which smoke detector should the people buy? Write **premium** or **basic** in your notebook.

1. Ms. Yu wants a long guarantee.
2. Phillip doesn't want to spend a lot of money.
3. Marilu doesn't want to stand on a chair to check her smoke alarm.

Giving Voice

Talk It Over

A. Everyone worries about keeping their families safe. What do you worry about? Tell your partner. Then tell the class.

B. Work with a small group. What can you do to keep your family safe? Make a list. Share your list with the class.

EXERCISE 5 Make Your Home Safer

A. A diagram is a simple drawing. A diagram is a good way to organize information about fire safety in your home. You can use a diagram to decide where to put smoke detectors. You can also use a diagram to show exits from your house in case of fire. Rachel Lubin and her three children live in a nice apartment on the third floor of a large apartment building. She made this diagram of her apartment. Answer the questions.

Diagram of Apartment

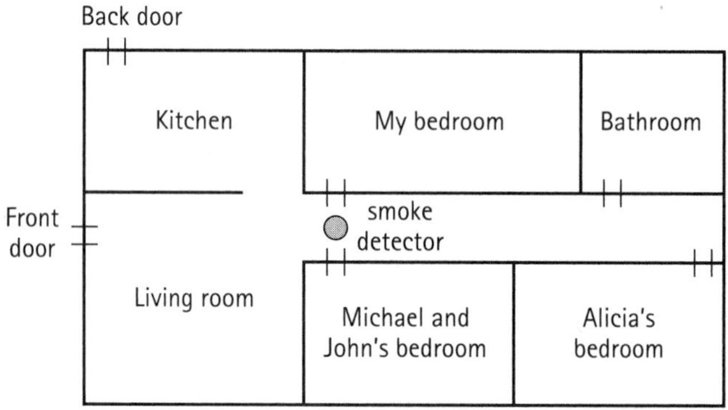

1. How many smoke detectors are in the apartment right now?
2. Does her family need another smoke detector? Where? Add the smoke detector to the drawing.
3. How can her family get out of the apartment in case of fire? Draw arrows to the doors. Can her family use the windows in case of fire? Why or why not?

B. Make a drawing of your house or apartment. Where do the smoke detectors go? Put them in the drawing. How can you get out in case of fire? Draw arrows.

LANGUAGE NOTE
Simple Conditions with *If*

We use simple conditions with **if** to talk about what we should do after another action happens.

> **If** the smoke alarm rings, you should go outside right away.

We use the simple present tense in the **if**-clause. We use the simple present, a command, **should, can, will,** or **have to** in the result clause.

> If the alarm **doesn't work**, you **should** check the battery
>
> **Go** outside right away if the smoke detector **rings.**

Review the article on page 88. Underline the sentences with simple conditions with **if.**

Accessing Information

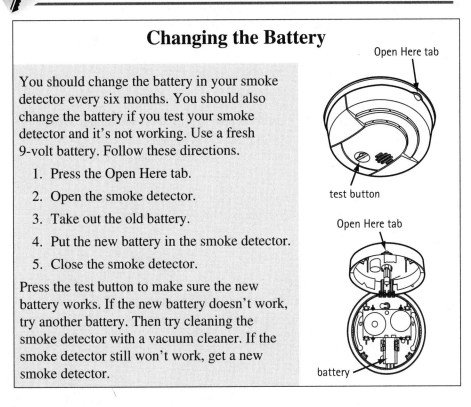

Changing the Battery

You should change the battery in your smoke detector every six months. You should also change the battery if you test your smoke detector and it's not working. Use a fresh 9-volt battery. Follow these directions.

1. Press the Open Here tab.
2. Open the smoke detector.
3. Take out the old battery.
4. Put the new battery in the smoke detector.
5. Close the smoke detector.

Press the test button to make sure the new battery works. If the new battery doesn't work, try another battery. Then try cleaning the smoke detector with a vacuum cleaner. If the smoke detector still won't work, get a new smoke detector.

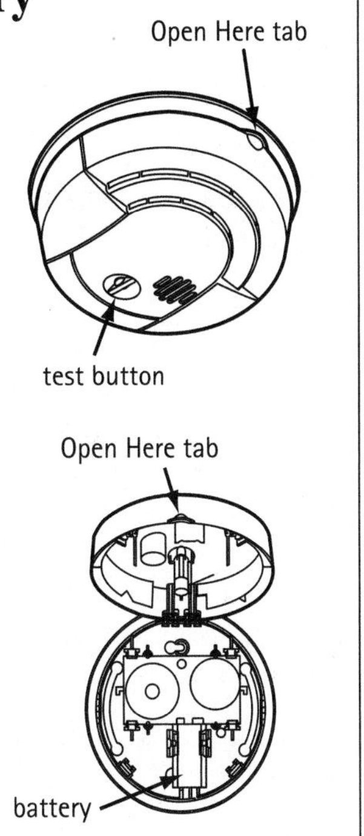

Talk About It

Work with a partner. Take turns telling each other how to change the battery in a smoke detector.

You Decide

How can you remember to check your smoke detector every month? Tell your partner. Share your partner's idea with the class.

EXERCISE 6 What Should They Do?

Read the problem. What should the people do? Write the answer in your notebook.

1. Mr. Gonzalez can't hear very well. His new apartment doesn't have a smoke detector.
2. Soo-ha tested her smoke detector. It's not working.
3. Carla's smoke detector looks old, but she doesn't know how old it is. It was in the apartment when she moved in six years ago.

READING STRATEGY
Skim for the Main Idea

When we skim, we read an article quickly in order to find the main idea. When we skim, we do these things:

1. We look at the drawings and pictures.
2. We read the title and the headings.
3. Then we read the rest of the article very quickly.

As we skim, we try to figure out the main idea. Once we know the main idea, we can do several things: We can use the main idea to figure out if the reading is important to us. If the main idea is important to us, we can reread the article more carefully. If it's not important, we can use the time to read something that is more important.

If we decide to read the article, we can use the main idea to help us remember all our background knowledge. We think of everything we know about the topic. If we think about our background knowledge before we read, we usually understand the article better.

EXERCISE 7 Skimming

A. Try skimming the article on changing a smoke detector battery on page 91. Check the boxes as you complete the steps.

☐ Look at the drawings and pictures.

☐ Read the title and the headings, if any.

☐ Read the rest of the article very quickly.

B. Now talk with a partner. What's the main idea of the reading? What background knowledge do you know about this topic? Share your ideas with the class.

EXERCISE 8 Before You Read

A. Try skimming the article on pages 93 and 94. Work very quickly. Check the boxes as you complete the steps. Then write the main idea on the line.

☐ Look at the drawings and pictures.

☐ Read the title and the headings.

☐ Read the rest of the article very quickly.

Main Idea: ____

B. Work with a partner. Talk about your background knowledge about the main idea. Write as much as you know about this main idea on the lines.

____

____

____

CD 2 TRACK 6

Staying Safe in a Tornado

A tornado is an extremely dangerous storm. A tornado is a circular storm in the shape of a funnel. These storms have strong winds that can reach 250 miles per hour. They can destroy whole towns and move heavy cars and trucks. A single tornado can kill many people and cause millions of dollars in damage. For example, a tornado that hit Fort Worth, Texas, in 2002 killed four people, injured 89 more, and caused over $300 million in damage. The worst day of tornados was in 1925. Almost 700 people died in tornadoes that hit three states—Illinois, Missouri, and Indiana—on the same day.

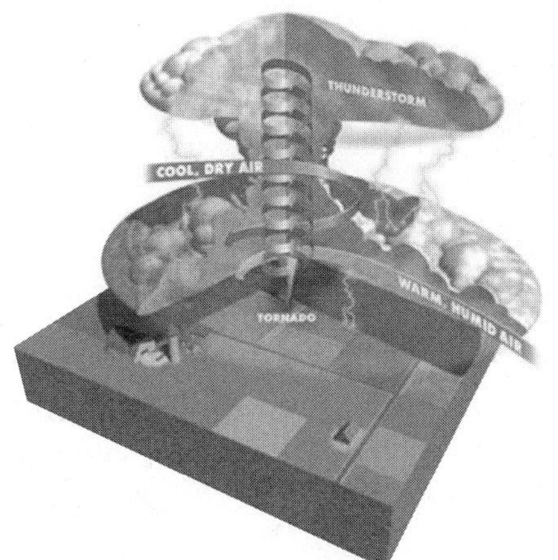

When and where do tornadoes happen?

The midwestern and southern states get the most tornados, but a tornado can happen in almost any part of the U.S. Spring and fall are the most common times of year for tornadoes.

How do tornadoes form?

A tornado forms when a large amount of hot air comes together with a large amount of cold air during a thunderstorm. The warm air begins to move up and in a circle, and the cool air starts moving down and in a circle. If the air begins moving very quickly, a tornado forms.

How do I know a tornado is coming?

Many cities, especially those in areas where tornadoes are common, have tornado alarms. If a tornado occurs in your area, you may hear a loud siren. Schools also have tornado alarms that will sound if a tornado is in the area. If a bad thunderstorm begins and you are worried about a tornado, you should check the radio, TV, or Internet to see if there is a tornado watch or warning. A **tornado watch** means that it's possible that a tornado could form. During a tornado watch, you should check the weather report and the weather frequently in case a tornado forms. You should also figure out what to do in case a tornado forms. Make sure you know where your children are, and decide where you will go. When you hear a **tornado warning,** it means that someone has seen a tornado. Danger signs that a tornado is nearby include:

- The sky is a strange green color.
- Hail is falling.
- It suddenly stops raining, and there is a strange quiet.
- You hear a loud noise that sounds like a speeding train. (This means that a tornado is very close by.)

continued →

What do I do in case of a tornado?

If a tornado is near you, or if you see a tornado, you should take action immediately. If you are outdoors, go into the nearest strong building. If you are driving, stop driving and get indoors, too. If you see a tornado and can't get indoors, you should go to the lowest land you can find and lie down. You should never try to get away from a tornado by driving away from it. The tornado may suddenly change direction or another tornado may suddenly appear.

When you are indoors, go to the basement. If there isn't a basement, go to the lowest floor of the building. Don't take the elevator. Use the stairs. The safest area is any corner. Stay away from windows. Other safe areas are the bathroom and a closet. If possible, keep a radio or TV with you.

How can I stay prepared for a tornado or other emergency?

Every home should have an emergency kit with these items in it:

- A flashlight and fresh batteries
- A portable radio and fresh batteries
- A first aid kit
- Bottled water, some cans of food, and a can opener

Your family should also have a plan of what to do in case of emergency. Your children should know your phone number and the phone number of a friend or relative. Your family should also know safe places to go if a tornado strikes when you are not at home.

EXERCISE 9 After You Read

Review your answers to Exercise 8 on page 92. Did skimming and thinking about your background knowledge help you when you read the article? Share your ideas with the class.

EXERCISE 10 Answer the Questions

Write the answers in your notebook.

1. What is a tornado?
2. Why are tornados dangerous?
3. What is a tornado watch? What should you do in a tornado watch?
4. What is a tornado warning? What should you do in a tornado warning?
5. Where should you go if you see a tornado or hear that one is nearby?
6. What is one warning sign that a tornado is nearby?

EXERCISE 11 How Tornados Form

How do tornados form? Number the steps from 1 to 4.

_______ **a.** The air moves faster and faster.

_______ **b.** A mass of cold air meets a mass of hot air during a thunderstorm.

_______ **c.** A funnel cloud forms.

_______ **d.** The cold air begins to move down, and the hot air begins to move up.

EXERCISE 12 Are They Staying Safe?

Read about the people. Are they staying safe? Write **yes** or **no** in your notebook. If they are not staying safe, what should they do? Write a few words in your notebook.

1. Nadia was driving to work. She heard on the radio that someone had seen a tornado about a mile from where she was. She stopped driving and went into a nearby store. She and the employees went to the basement.
2. Jason was at school. All the children in the school went to the basement during the tornado warning. Later he heard that a tornado had struck downtown. He knew that his mother worked downtown, so he asked permission to call her at work. She was OK because everyone in the company was in the basement. However, the building she worked in was damaged.
3. Sonia was driving to the movies. She saw a tornado coming down the highway in front of her. She got off the highway and drove away from the storm. She kept driving until she was far away from the tornado.
4. Ron was working in a tall office building late at night. He heard that there was a tornado warning. He went to the top floor of the building to see if the tornado was nearby.
5. Jerry loves taking photographs. He saw a tornado a few miles away. He began taking pictures. He stayed outside taking pictures for 15 minutes.

Reading Journal

Complete a copy of the reading journal form on page 126. Keep the form in your notebook or portfolio.

Taking Action

A. What should your class do in case of a fire? A tornado? Find out your school's plans in case of a fire or a tornado.

B. Have a class fire drill. Follow the fire procedures you identified in part A. Talk about your experiences. Were you able to get out of the building quickly? Was everyone safe from danger? Later, have a class tornado drill.

Enriching Your Vocabulary

A tornado is just one kind of emergency. Study the vocabulary.
hurricane–dangerous storm that forms at sea. It has strong winds and is dangerous if it reaches land.
wildfire–large fire that is burning outdoors
earthquake–emergency in which the ground moves. Buildings can fall down and fires can start.
flood–emergency in which a lot of water is on the ground or in people's houses

Bridging to the Future

Tornadoes occur in every part of the U.S. However, they are more common in the Midwest and South. Look at the list in Enriching Your Vocabulary. Which of these are problems where you live? Work with a group. Choose one of the dangers. What should you and your family do in case it strikes? Then make a plan. Share your plan with the class.

Workplace Connection

What should you do at your workplace in case of a fire, a tornado, or another kind of danger? Does your workplace ever have drills, such as a fire or tornado drill? What happens? Where do you go? What do you do? Share your answers with a partner.

STUDY SKILL
Highlighting Important Information

When you read, a good way to learn the most important information is by using a highlighter. A highlighter is a special marker that you can use to mark the information with color. Then, when you review the information for a test, you just review the information that is highlighted. You can buy highlighters in colors such as yellow, blue, or pink. If you don't like highlighters, you can also underline information with a colored pen.

Review

EXERCISE 13 Answer the Questions

A. Skim the article. Look at the picture. Read the title. Read the rest of the information very quickly. Then write the main idea on the line.

Main Idea: ______________________________

B. Think about your background knowledge about the main idea. Write as much as you know about this main idea in your notebook. Then reread the information.

Staying Safe from Lightning

Lightning is a strong bolt of electricity that forms during a thunderstorm. Lightning can be very dangerous if it hits you or a building you are in.

Tips on staying safe in a lightning storm.

- If you are outdoors, try to get into your car or indoors as quickly as possible.
- If you can't get indoors, don't stand under trees. The lightning may hit the tree. Instead, go to low ground.

Once you are indoors, follow these tips:

- Stay indoors. Don't go outside until the storm passes.
- Avoid using the telephone or taking a bath until the storm passes.

EXERCISE 14 Answer the Questions

Write the answers in your notebook.

1. You drove to the park with your friends. You see lightning nearby. What do you do?
2. You're talking on the telephone. A bad thunderstorm begins. There is a lot of lightning. What do you do?

Your Portfolio

Review the plan you wrote in Bridging to the Future on page 96. Put a copy of your plan in your portfolio.

Summing Up

I can:

- ☐ **1.** Read about smoke detectors.
- ☐ **2.** Read about what to do in case of a tornado.
- ☐ **3.** Skim for the main idea.
- ☐ **4.** Understand simple conditions with **if.**
- ☐ **5.** Use a diagram to organize information.
- ☐ **6.** ______________________________

Fun and Relaxation

In this unit, you will:

1. Read about a famous folk song.
2. Read about a famous singer.
3. Distinguish between fact and opinion.
4. Understand linking verbs.
5. Use a scale to show agreement.

Accessing Information

Talk About It

Where are the people? What are they doing? What kinds of music are they singing?

You Decide

What kind of music do you like? Who's your favorite singer? Why?

Key Vocabulary

A. In this unit, you will read about music. First you will read about a famous folk song and the musician who wrote it. Then you will read about one of the most important salsa singers in the world. First, work with a partner. In your notebook, write a list of words you know about music.

B. Study the vocabulary.

redwood tree

land–the part of earth where people live; also, a country

island–small piece of land with water on all sides

poverty–being poor

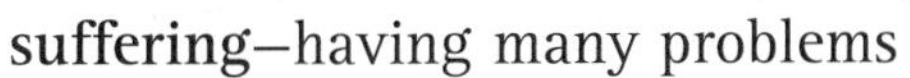

suffering–having many problems

influence–someone or something that affects you a lot or changes you

talent–something you are good at

popular–liked by a lot of people

EXERCISE 1 Vocabulary

Write the word from Key Vocabulary, part B on the line.

1. Alfredo is an excellent piano player. He has a lot of ____________________.
2. Miss Werner was my best teacher. She was a big ____________________ on my life.
3. ____________________ are amazing. These huge plants grow in California.
4. New York City is on an ____________________. On the west side is the Hudson River. On the other side is the East River.
5. There is a lot of ____________________ in my town because many people don't have jobs.

EXERCISE 2 Before You Read

The article on page 100 is about Woody Guthrie, a singer and the author of a famous song. As you read the article, figure out the author's opinions about Woody Guthrie and the song. Write a few words on the lines.

Guthrie: ____

The song: ____

What is a folk song?

CD 2 TRACK 7

Guthrie, Woody 1912–1967

Woody Guthrie: American Folksinger and Songwriter

Folksinger and music writer Woody Guthrie is the author of one of the most loved folk songs, "This Land Is Your Land." This song is simple, but the words are powerful. The song talks about places and things people love, such as the huge redwood trees in California and the warm waters of the Gulf of Mexico.

A folk song is a song that is "from the people." Every culture has folk songs. Usually, they are quiet, simple songs. People often sing them with just a guitar or a few other instruments. Some folk songs are so old that no one knows who wrote them or when they were written. Other folk songs are by songwriters who are interested in people's lives and experiences. Woody Guthrie was one of those songwriters.

Woody Guthrie was born in a very small town in Oklahoma in 1912. Guthrie first learned to play the guitar from his grandfather in 1917. He soon began to perform with other people in the area. People liked his music and encouraged him to perform.

After the Great Depression began in 1929, the economy was bad. Many people were not working, and there were many poor people. On top of that, weather was terrible in Oklahoma, and farmers lost their money and land. Guthrie's family lost everything. Guthrie began to travel around the country looking for work. Everywhere he went, he saw that the Depression caused poverty and suffering. Guthrie became interested in singing about people and their problems.

In the winter of 1940, Guthrie decided to go to New York. On his way, he composed "This Land Is Your Land." The song is about places and things he saw during his travels around the U.S.–such as tall trees in California. The last line of the song says, "This land was made for you and me." These words remind us that everyone is equal.

Woody Guthrie died in 1967, but his music lives on. He was given a place in the Rock and Roll Hall of Fame in 1988. Woody Guthrie never won a Grammy award. However, his music is an important part of American history and culture. In 2000, Guthrie received a Lifetime Achievement Award from the Grammys. Many popular singers such as Bono and Bruce Springsteen say that Woody Guthrie's music was a big influence on them. And to this day, people love to sing this favorite folk song.

This Land Is Your Land©
By Woody Guthrie

This land is your land,
This land is my land,
from California to the New York island
From the redwood forest to the Gulf Stream waters
This land was made for you and me,

EXERCISE 3 After You Read

A. Review your answer to Exercise 2 on page 99. What is the writer's opinion about Guthrie and the song "This Land Is Your Land"? Why do you think so?

B. Answer the questions. Write the answers in your notebook.

1. Do you agree with the writer's opinion of Guthrie? Why or why not?
2. Do you agree with the writer's opinion of the song? Why or why not?

EXERCISE 4 Answer the Questions

Write the answers in your notebook.

1. What is a folk song?
2. What was the Great Depression?
3. How did the Depression affect Woody Guthrie? How did it affect his music?
4. What is the last line of the song? Why is it important?
5. When did Woody Guthrie die?
6. Is Woody Guthrie's music important today? Why?

Teamwork

Work with a partner. Student A says the song on page 100 aloud. Student B finds the places on the map on page 125. Then switch roles and repeat the activity.

EXERCISE 5 Using a Scale to Show Agreement

A. We may agree or disagree with an opinion. When we agree with an opinion, we may agree strongly or not very strongly. A good way to show how we agree with an opinion is by rating our opinion on a scale. Look at the statement and the scale. Does the person agree with the statement? How strongly?

	Disagree			Agree
Guthrie was a good songwriter.	1	2	3	(4)

B. Rate your agreement with the statements. Circle the number.

	Disagree			Agree
1. It's fun to listen to music.	1	2	3	4
2. Listening to music is relaxing.	1	2	3	4
3. Listening to music is a good hobby.	1	2	3	4

Giving Voice

Talk It Over

A. Folk music is just one kind of music. There are many other kinds of music, such as rock, hip-hop, rap, jazz, blues, and classical music. Work with a partner. Which of these do you like? Can you name any singers or song titles? Write a few words in your notebook. Share your ideas with the class.

B. Work with a partner. What other kinds of music do you like? Write your ideas in your notebook. Include music from your culture. Describe the music. What does it sound like? What are the words about? Share your ideas with the class.

EXERCISE 6 Survey

A. Think about the kinds of music you discussed in Talk It Over. Which ones are the most popular in your class? Work with a partner. Write five questions. Then survey everyone in your class using a scale. Follow the example.

	Disagree			Agree
I like to listen to classical music.	1	2	3	4

B. Share your results with the rest of the class. What is the most popular kind of music? The least popular? Why do you think so? Share your ideas with the class.

Enriching Your Vocabulary

We use a lot of different equipment to listen to music. Study the vocabulary.

CD player

personal stereo

DVD player

headphones

cassette player

What equipment do you use to listen to music? Tell your partner. Share your partner's ideas with the class.

Accessing Information

One of the best American folk songs is "I've Been Working on the Railroad." This song became popular during the 19th century when workers were building the first train lines from the eastern part of the U.S. to California. Building the first railroads was hard work. In summer the sun burned down, and in winter ice-cold winds blew. To make the work easier, the workers sang as they worked. Because there were no radios, TVs, or movies, they also sang for entertainment at night. One of the songs they liked the most was this one:

I've Been Working on the Railroad

I've been working on the railroad
All the live long day.
I've been working on the railroad
Just to pass the time away.
Can't you hear the whistle blowing?
Rise up so early in the morn.
Can't you hear the captain shouting,
Dinah, blow your horn.

In the song, the workers complain about working hard and getting up early for work. When they had to get up, the train whistle would blow to tell them to get up.

Talk About It

What's the name of the song? Who sang the song? Why did they sing it? Do you ever feel like the workers in the song? Do you know how to sing the song? Folk music is about the life of common, or average, people. Is this song a true folk song? Why?

You Decide

What other folk songs do you know? What are they about?

READING STRATEGY
Distinguish Between Fact and Opinion

Readings have both facts and opinions. A fact is a piece of information that is true. We can check a fact to make sure it's accurate. For example, it's a fact that Woody Guthrie was born in 1912. It's also a fact that he learned to play the guitar from his grandfather.

An opinion is something that people believe. An opinion may or may not be true. People may disagree about an opinion. For example, it's an opinion that "This Land Is Your Land" is an excellent song.

When we read, it's important to figure out which information is a fact and which information is the author's opinion. If we have questions about the facts, we can check them to make sure they are true. If information is an opinion, we can decide whether or not we agree with the opinion.

EXERCISE 7 Fact or Opinion?

A. Read the sentences. Which ones are facts? Check the boxes.

- ☐ **1.** Woody Guthrie was a folksinger.
- ☐ **2.** "This Land Is Your Land" is a wonderful song for children.
- ☐ **3.** Guthrie wrote "This Land Is Your Land" in 1940.
- ☐ **4.** Everyone should know "This Land Is Your Land."
- ☐ **5.** Woody Guthrie is the best folksinger in the world.
- ☐ **6.** The Great Depression began in 1929.
- ☐ **7.** ______________________________
- ☑ **8.** ______________________________

B. Review the items that are opinions. Do you agree with them? Why or why not? Talk over your opinions with a partner. Share your ideas with the class.

EXERCISE 8 Facts and Opinions

Review the article on "I've Been Working on the Railroad" on page 103. Write one fact and one opinion about the song in your notebook.

EXERCISE 9 Before You Read

The article on pages 105 and 106 is about a famous singer. As you read the article, find one fact and one opinion. Underline the fact. Circle the opinion.

Why is Celia Cruz so popular?

CD 2 TRACK 8

Celia Cruz, Queen of Salsa

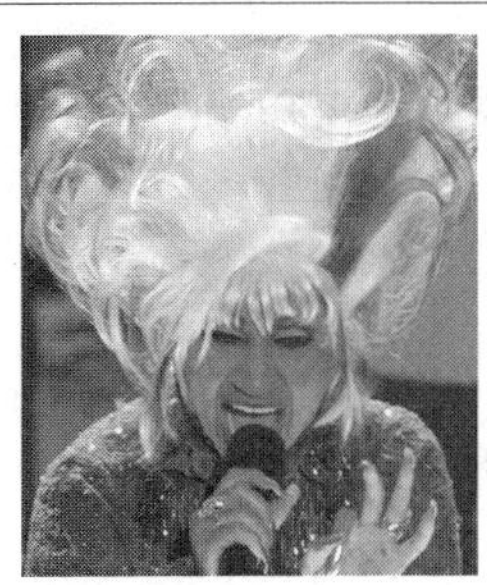

Salsa is a type of music that started in Cuba, Puerto Rico, and the Dominican Republic. Salsa music is loud and exciting. Salsa sounds hot and spicy. One of the most important salsa singers in the world was Celia Cruz.

Childhood and Growing Up

Celia Cruz was born in about 1924 into a poor family in Cuba. Fourteen children lived in her home, and sometimes there was not a lot of money for food. From a very young age, Cruz loved music and showed a talent for it. When she sang to her brothers and sisters at bedtime, neighbors would listen.

When she was 14 years old, Cruz started entering and winning singing contests. The prizes were often food. In 2000, she said, "I really loved to sing. But I also did it because if you won, you would get a cake, or a bag with chocolate, condensed milk .... We were very poor. And all of that came in very handy at home."

Her Career in Music

Cruz's family loved her music, and they encouraged her to sing. However, her father wanted her to become a teacher, so she started to study education. But her teachers saw her talent and encouraged her to sing. Soon she changed schools and began to study at a famous music school, the National Conservatory of Music in Havana. She continued to sing on the radio and in contests. Then a band leader hired her to sing with his band. At first, people did not like her voice. Cruz said that at that time her voice sounded very different from later—her voice seemed very high then. And people weren't used to seeing a woman sing. But little by little people accepted her, and she became more and more popular. She soon became the best salsa singer in Cuba.

During this time, a record company wanted her band to make a record. But the president of the company said that people didn't want to hear a woman singing salsa. He thought the band should make the record without Celia Cruz. But the leader of the band believed in Cruz's talent. He said that he would pay for the record if it wasn't successful. The record was a hit. By the 1950s, Celia Cruz was a famous singer in Cuba and was beginning to become famous in other countries as well.

Moving to the U.S.

In 1960, Celia Cruz moved to the U.S., and after many years of hard work, she started to become famous in the U.S. as well. At first, she was popular with immigrants from Cuba and other countries. But as time went on, she became popular with a wider audience. She made over 70 recordings and performed with many important singers and dancers. She gave concerts around the U.S. and in many other countries, including Sweden, Germany, Japan, England, and Morocco. She always worked very hard. Usually she toured the world for 11 months of the year, spending hundreds of hours on airplanes. She also made several movies.

Even though performing was hard work, Celia Cruz said that she loved it. In a 2002 interview, she said, "My life is singing. I can have a headache, but when it's time to sing and I step on that stage, there is no more headache." Celia Cruz wore fancy, colorful dresses and huge wigs that looked as tall as trees. She was also famous for her dancing.

continued →

The Importance of Her Work

Celia Cruz's work is important in many ways. She was the first woman to become a popular salsa singer, and she was one of the first female Hispanic singers to become a star in the U.S. Her work was a big influence on later performers such as Gloria Estefan and Selena. Celia Cruz also did a lot to encourage younger performers. She started the Celia Cruz Foundation, which helps young musicians pay for their music studies. She also raised money to fight cancer. During her life, she received many awards and prizes. She won five Grammy Awards and two Latin Grammy Awards, as well as prizes from various governments from around the world. In 1997, she received the National Medal of Arts from then president Bill Clinton.

Sadly, Celia Cruz died of cancer on July 16, 2003. People will always remember her beautiful music and exciting performances.

EXERCISE 10 After You Read

Share your answers to Exercise 9 on page 104 with the class. Do you agree with the opinion? Why or why not? Tell the class.

EXERCISE 11 Answer the Questions

Write the answers in your notebook.

1. What is salsa? What is it like?
2. What was Celia Cruz's family like?
3. Why did she enter singing contests?
4. What problems did she have at the beginning of her career?
5. When did she move to the U.S.?
6. Was she successful after she moved to the U.S.? How do you know?

EXERCISE 12 Fact or Opinion?

Write **fact** or **opinion** on the line.

________ 1. Salsa music started in Puerto Rico, Cuba, and the Dominican Republic.

________ 2. Women shouldn't be salsa singers.

________ 3. Celia Cruz's first record was a hit.

________ 4. Celia Cruz's performances were always exciting.

________ 5. Celia Cruz performed in Morocco.

________ 6. Celia Cruz made over 70 recordings.

EXERCISE 13 Compare and Contrast

A. Compare and contrast Cruz's music with Guthrie's music. Check the box or boxes.

		Guthrie	Cruz
1.	Loud and exciting	☐	☐
2.	Quiet and simple	☐	☐
3.	Sung with a large band	☐	☐
4.	Sung with one or two instruments, such as a guitar	☐	☐
5.	Popular with many people	☐	☐
6.	Influenced other singers and songwriters	☐	☐
7.	Won important prizes	☐	☐

B. A Venn diagram is a good way to compare and contrast information. Write the numbers from part A in the Venn diagram.

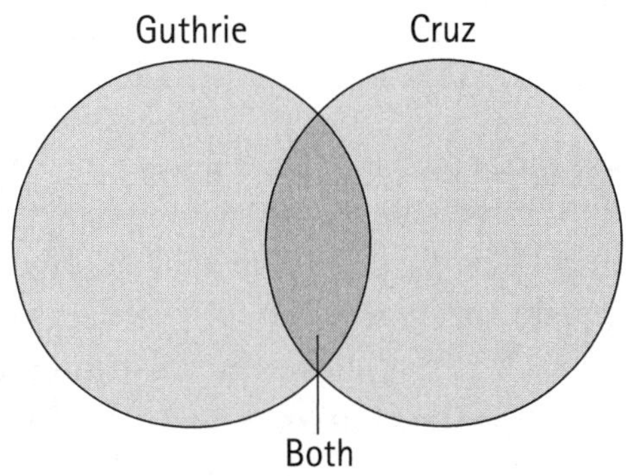

LANGUAGE NOTE
Linking Verbs

We use linking verbs when we describe. The most common linking verb is **be (am, is, are).** Other common linking verbs are **look, sound, smell,** and **taste.** Study the examples.

That music **sounds** beautiful.

Roberta won't eat food that **tastes** spicy.

Review the article on pages 105 and 106. Circle the linking verbs.

Reading Journal

Complete a copy of the reading journal form on page 126. Keep the form in your notebook or portfolio.

Taking Action

A. A lot of folk music is about people's problems. What are some of the problems people have today? Work with a partner and make a list.

B. Review the ideas you gathered in Taking Action, part A. With a partner or a small group, write a song, a poem, a story, or a letter to the editor of a local newspaper about one of the problems. For example, you might write a song about a bad day. Share your writing with the class.

A Bad Day

I stand at the bus stop
Rain pouring down.
Feeling sad because work was hard today.
Wishing I could take a cab.
Why doesn't it rain money
Instead of raindrops that wet my head?

Bridging to the Future

Woody Guthrie and Celia Cruz had special talents. They used their talents to make music that everyone will remember. What special talents do you have? Write one of your best talents in your notebook. How can you develop your talent? Write a few ideas in your notebook.

Family Connection

Celia Cruz and Woody Guthrie became interested in music because of their families, friends, and teachers. What are your family's interests in music? How can you help your family become more interested in music? Share your ideas with the class.

STUDY SKILL

Relaxing When You Study

Experts say that we learn better when we are relaxed. But people relax in different ways. One good way for people to stay relaxed when they study is to sit in a comfortable chair. Other people like to listen to music. Other people like to chew gum. What helps you relax when you study? Tell the class. Then use it to help you stay relaxed when you study.

Review

EXERCISE 14 Answer the Questions

A. Write the answers in your notebook.

The Music Video

Entertainment has changed a lot since the time of Woody Guthrie. One of the biggest changes is the music video. A music video is a short movie of a singer or band performing a song. Watching a music video, we can see colorful, entertaining pictures as we listen to the music. Often the pictures tell the story of the song or help us understand the song in a new way. However, some people don't like music videos. They think that many music videos are violent. They also think that people spend too much time watching music videos. Other people say that videos make music more enjoyable. Because of videos, music has changed forever.

1. What is a music video?
2. Where can we see them?
3. How do music videos help us understand songs?
4. Why do some people dislike music videos?

B. Review the article. Write one fact and one opinion on the lines.

Fact: ____________________

Opinion: ____________________

Your Portfolio

Review your answer to part B of Taking Action on page 108. Put a copy in your portfolio.

Summing Up

I can:

- [ ] **1.** Read about a famous folk song.
- [ ] **2.** Read about a famous singer.
- [ ] **3.** Distinguish between fact and opinion.
- [ ] **4.** Understand linking verbs.
- [ ] **5.** Use a scale to show agreement.
- [ ] **6.** ____________________

UNIT 10

Lifelong Learning

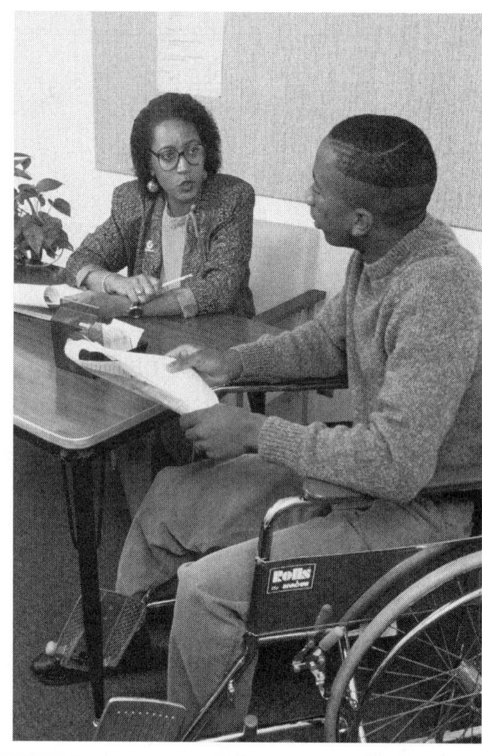

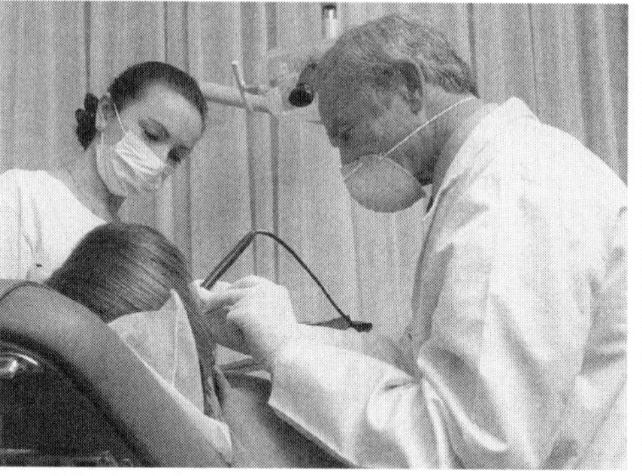

In this unit, you will:

1. Read about jobs that are growing in number.
2. Read about teaching children about work.
3. Understand cause-effect relationships.
4. Understand the future tense with **will.**
5. Use a chart to organize information.

Accessing Information

Talk About It

What are the people doing?
What are they saying?

You Decide

How can you find a better job?

Key Vocabulary

A. In this unit, you will read about jobs that are growing in number right now. Then you will read about a special event that teaches children about the workplace. First, work with a partner. In your notebook, write a list of words you know about work.

B. Study the vocabulary.

assistant–employee whose job is helping another person

vocational-technical school–school where people get training for technical jobs, such as auto repair, heating and air conditioning, hairdressing, etc.

successful–having good results

career–the area you work in for most of your life

training–learning how to do a job

require–make necessary

high school diploma–document that says that you finished high school

EXERCISE 1 Vocabulary

Write the word from Key Vocabulary, part B on the line.

1. In order to get this job, you have to have a ____________________ or a GED.
2. No special ____________________ is necessary to get a job as a sandwich maker.
3. A dental ____________________ helps a dentist.
4. To become an auto mechanic, you can go to school at a ____________________.
5. That job ____________________ two years of study at a community college.
6. If you find a job you like and work hard at it, you can have a ____________________ career.

EXERCISE 2 Before You Read

When we read, we often look for cause-effect relationships. The article on the next page is about jobs and how to get them. As you read the article, figure out the relationship between education and pay.

Where can you find a good job?

CD 2 TRACK 9

Top Jobs for the Next 10 Years

Are you looking for a job? Do you want to find a better job? Or are you worried about losing your job and finding another one? Experts say that a good way to find a good job is to look in areas that are growing. The U.S. government has gathered information on the jobs that are growing the fastest. Here are six jobs from the top of the list.

• **Medical Assistant**
Medical assistants help doctors and patients. They answer phones, get information from patients, and complete paperwork. They also help with medical tests, take temperatures, and weigh patients. The pay is good, and one to two years of training at a community college or a vocational-technical school are required.

• **Hotel Desk Clerk**
Hotel desk clerks help guests check in, keep track of which rooms are empty, solve problems for guests, and take payments when guests check out. Most of these workers get their training on-the-job. Hotel workers have to be very neat and punctual. They also have to get along with people. These jobs are easy to find. The pay is average.

• **Customer Service Representative**
These workers work for different kinds of companies including gas and electric companies, banks, credit card companies, and airlines. They take orders over the phone, answer questions, and solve problems for customers. Many companies need customer service representatives with skills in English and another language. These jobs are easy to find and the training is on-the-job. The pay is average.

• **Personal and Home Care Aides**
These aides help elderly and disabled adults in their homes or in nursing homes. Aides help with cleaning, cooking meals, and other home care tasks. They also help adults get dressed, go to medical appointments, and visit friends. Most aides need only on-the-job training. It's easy to find one of these jobs, but the pay is low.

• **Social and Human Service Assistants**
These workers find social services for adults and children. They help families solve problems by finding medical care, special transit, home health care, home personal care, and so on. It's easy to get one of these jobs, but employers require one to two years of study in a community college. The pay is average.

• **Teacher Assistant**
A teacher assistant helps a teacher so the teacher can spend more time with students. Teacher assistants correct homework, complete paperwork, watch children in the cafeteria and playground, and get equipment ready. Some schools require a high school diploma or a GED. Other schools require some college. The pay is good, but these jobs are hard to find.

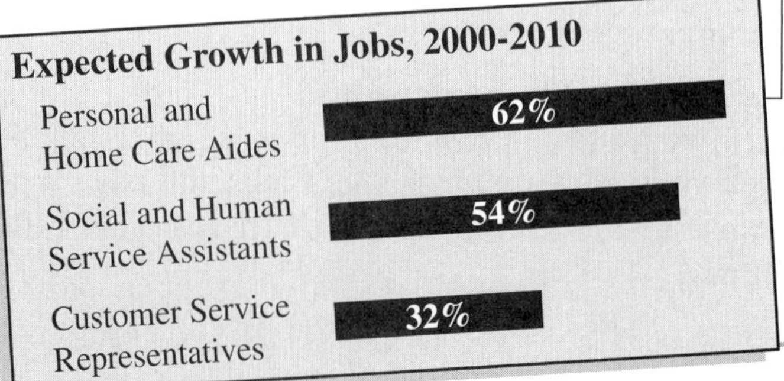

EXERCISE 3 After You Read

Review your answer to Exercise 2 on page 111. What's the relationship between education and pay? Share your answers with the class.

EXERCISE 4 Answer the Questions

Write the answers in your notebook.

1. What do medical assistants do?
2. Where do hotel desk clerks get their training?
3. Why do hotel desk clerks need to get along with people?
4. Which job is good for people who speak two languages?
5. Which job is good for people who like children?
6. Which jobs require the most education?
7. Which job requires cooking skills?

EXERCISE 5 Complete the Chart

Complete the chart about jobs in your notebook. Follow the example. Use the information in the article on page 112.

Job Title	Training or Education Required	Pay
Medical Assistant	one to two years at a community college or vocational-technical school	good

Teamwork

A. Work with a partner. Student A looks at the information on Growth in Jobs on page 112. Student B looks at the information on page 125. Ask your partner questions such as, "What's the expected growth in jobs for (medical assistants)?" Complete the chart.

Expected Growth in Jobs, 2000–2010	%
Teacher Assistants	
Hotel Desk Clerks	
Medical Assistants	

B. Review your answers to part A and to Exercise 5. Which jobs are growing the fastest? Are you interested in any of the jobs? Why or why not? Tell your ideas to your partner. Share your partner's ideas with the class.

Giving Voice

Talk It Over

A. Work with a small group. Read the list of jobs. Do you know what training is needed for each of them? Do workers need on-the-job training, vocational-technical school, a high school diploma or GED, a community college degree, or a college or university degree? Talk over your ideas. If necessary, check in the library. Write your answers in your notebook.

1. barber/hairdresser
2. cashier
3. dental assistant
4. waiter/waitress
5. janitor
6. teacher
7. engineer
8. auto mechanic
9. telephone repair person
10. video clerk
11. electrician
12. bus driver

B. The reading on page 112 is about jobs that are growing. Which of the jobs in part A are growing? Why do you think so? What are some other jobs that are growing? Why do you think so? What are some jobs that are becoming less important? Why do you think so? Work with a small group and answer the questions. Share your answers with the class.

EXERCISE 6 What Training Do You Need?

Work with a partner. Review your answers to Talk It Over. What can you do to get one of the growing jobs? Will you need more education? More training? Better English skills? Choose a job for each of you and make a list of things you can do to get the job. Share the job and your list with the class.

Enriching Your Vocabulary

Computer technology has created many new jobs.

computer programmer—developer of new programs for computers

online instructor—teacher of Internet classes

computer trainer—trainer of people to use computers or new computer programs

computer technician—worker who installs and repairs computers

Web designer—designer of Internet Web pages

Webmaster—person who is in charge of a Web site on the Internet

What special training do people need to get these jobs? Where can they get this training? Talk over your ideas with the class.

Accessing Information

Lake View Mall JOB FAIR

Lake View Mall is opening soon. Over 125 new stores need managers and employees. Here are some of the hundreds of new jobs you can interview for:

- cooks
- security guards
- cashiers
- hairdressers
- barbers
- store managers
- restaurant managers
- photo clerks
- photo managers
- payroll clerks
- payroll managers
- auto mechanics
- janitors
- pharmacists
- pharmacy clerks
- waiters and waitresses
- mail clerks
- gardeners
- heating and cooling technicians
- computer technicians
- salespeople
- pet store clerks

The job fair is Saturday, October 25, from 10:00 AM to 3:00 PM at Kennedy High School. Dress for success!

Kennedy High School
1111 N. Kennedy Drive
Lake View

Talk About It

What is a job fair? What do people do at a job fair? What should you do to prepare for a job fair? What should you bring? What does it mean to dress for success?

You Decide

You're going to the job fair. What jobs do you want to apply for? Why? What will you wear? Why?

READING STRATEGY
Understand Cause-Effect Relationships

A cause makes something happen. The things that happen because of a cause are the effects. For example, imagine that you are a clerk at a computer store. You take classes in computer repair at the community college. As a result, you get a promotion. Completing the classes is the cause. The promotion is the effect.

Sometimes, a cause can have more than one effect. For example, in addition to a promotion, you also get a raise. A result can also be the cause of additional effects. For example, because you got a raise and a promotion, you decide to take more classes at the community college.

EXERCISE 7 Causes and Effects

Think about the reading on page 115. What is one cause for attending the job fair? What is one possible effect of attending the job fair? Write a few words on the lines. Share your ideas with the class.

Cause: ______________________________

Effect: ______________________________

EXERCISE 8 What Are the Effects?

Read the causes. Write two possible effects in your notebook.

1. You get a raise.
2. You buy a car.
3. You find out that your company is going to close.
4. A nice new supermarket just opened near your house.
5. You complete a training class at work.
6. You catch a bad cold.
7. A relative comes to visit you.
8. You find out that you have to work on Thanksgiving.

EXERCISE 9 Before You Read

The reading on the next page is about Take Our Daughters and Sons to Work Day. It's a special event that helps parents teach their children about work. As you read the article, put a check mark next to each effect of Take Our Daughters and Sons to Work Day.

CD 2 TRACK 10

Take Our Daughters and Sons to Work Day

Parents worry about their jobs and careers. But parents also worry about their children's futures. "Will my children get the education and training they need? Will they be able to find good jobs? Will they find careers they like?" One of the best ways to start answering these questions is through National Take Our Daughters and Sons to Work Day®.

Take Our Daughters and Sons to Work Day is a national event that is celebrated in many companies around the U.S. It's over ten years old, and it usually takes place on the fourth Thursday in April. Some companies, however, have the event in summer when children are not in school.

On Take Our Daughters and Sons to Work Day, many companies invite their employees to bring their children to work with them. The children can find out about their parents' jobs, see how the company works, and meet the people their parents spend the day with. There are also special events for the families. Many times, the head of the company will speak to the children. Sometimes, the children will see a movie about the company, and different workers will talk to the children about the company, their jobs, and the company's products. There is often a welcome breakfast, a special meal at lunch, or ice cream at the end of the day.

Take Our Daughters and Sons to Work Day has a number of benefits. First, children find out about work. They learn what workplaces are like. In addition, the children grow closer to their parents because they understand their parents' lives better. Parents like this day because their coworkers get to find out about their families. Bosses and coworkers understand employees better after they meet the employees' children. After Take Our Daughters and Sons to Work Day, parents and children both say that they feel proud of each other. And, even more important, Take Our Daughters and Sons to Work Day is fun. Parents and children don't often get to spend a lot of time together these days, and this special event lets them spend an entire day together.

For example, last year Albert Wu took his son and daughter to his workplace. Albert is the manager of a popular restaurant. The children, Michael, age 12, and Lydia, age 9, had never been to the restaurant before. They got to see their father's workplace for the first time. They also got to try the food at the restaurant, and one of the cooks showed them how he prepares food for customers. Michael and Lydia were lucky, too. They got to see a famous actor who came to the restaurant for lunch. They also saw their father working very hard taking care of customers. Michael said, "Now I know why my dad is tired when he gets home." Albert said, "During the day, I talked to my children about work. Now I know the kinds of jobs they are interested in. My children also know what work is like. They will be ready to get good jobs. And my coworkers know two of the most important people in my life—my children."

Not all companies celebrate this day. Workers with difficult or dangerous jobs may not be able to participate. But if your company offers Take Our Daughters and Sons to Work Day, talk to your boss about participating in it. If your children will miss school, talk to their teachers. Make sure the children won't miss a test. Find out the children's homework so they can do it when they get home.

continued 

If your company doesn't offer Take Our Daughters and Sons to Work Day, the fourth Thursday in April is still a good time to talk to your children about work. Talk with them about your job and career. Talk about what you do at work, what your boss is like, how you got your job, and things you are doing to get a better job. Find out which jobs your children are interested in. Then help them use the Internet or the library to find out more about the jobs and the education and training required to get them. For older children, find out when their schools offer career fairs or career days. Then encourage them to attend, or go with them.

Whether you take your children to work or simply talk to them about work, you will help prepare them for successful careers.

EXERCISE 10 After You Read

Review your answers to Exercise 9 on page 116. What are the effects of Take Our Daughters and Sons to Work Day? Do you think that an event like this one is a good idea? Why or why not? Share your answers with the class.

STUDY SKILL
Using a Dictionary

One of the best tools for studying is a dictionary. A dictionary is organized in alphabetical order. To find a word, you look at the guide words at the top of the page. The guide words tell you the first and last words on that page. That way, you don't have to look at every word on the page to find out if the word you are looking for is on that page.

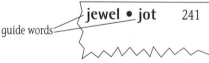

guide words — **jewel • jot** 241

The dictionary entry for each word usually has the pronunciation and the various definitions of a word.

word — **job** /jäb/ *noun* — pronunciation

definitions:
1 work that you do for money
2 a piece of work

When you find a word you don't know, you should use a dictionary if you can't figure out the word's meaning from the context. If you can skip the word and still understand the main idea of the reading, you shouldn't use a dictionary.

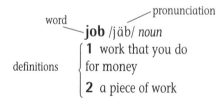

EXERCISE 11 Answer the Questions

Write the answers in your notebook.

1. When is Take Our Daughters and Sons to Work Day?
2. What do many companies do on this day?
3. What do children learn from this day?
4. Who is Albert Wu? What did he do on Take Our Daughters and Sons to Work Day?
5. Did this day help his family? How do you know?
6. Can all workers take their children to work? Why? Give two reasons.
7. What can parents do if they can't participate in Take Our Daughters and Sons to Work Day?

EXERCISE 12 What Did They Learn?

A. What were the effects of Take Our Daughters and Sons to Work Day? Complete the chart.

People	Effects
Michael and Lydia Wu	
Albert Wu	
Albert's coworkers	

B. Work with a partner. Was Take Our Daughters and Sons to Work Day a good experience for the family? Why do you think so? Share your ideas with your partner. Share your partner's ideas with the class.

LANGUAGE NOTE
Future Tense with *Will*

We use the future tense with **will** to talk about future plans. The short form of **will** is **'ll.**

Usually, the head of the company **will** speak to the children.

Review the article on pages 117 and 118. Circle the examples of **will.**

Reading Journal

Complete a copy of the reading journal form on page 126. Keep the form in your notebook or portfolio.

Taking Action

A. Often, the best sources of information about jobs are the people you know. Work as a group. Each student should prepare a card about his or her workplace or a workplace he or she knows about. The card should include information about the company, jobs available at the company, and the training needed. Follow the example.

Vacation Hotel
1000 Beach Road
Sarasota, FL 34680

Job	Training
Desk Clerk	*On-the-job*
Housekeeper	*On-the-job*
Manager	*Two years of community college*

B. Work as a class. Each student reads his or her card aloud and answers questions from the class. Put all the cards in a place where everyone can refer to them.

Bridging to the Future

Work in a group. A local school has asked your group to speak to a group of children about ways to succeed at work. What information do you include in the talk? Why? Prepare a list of information that you want to present to the children. Then prepare a talk of about ten minutes. Your group should present its talk to the rest of the class. Then talk about the information your class presented. How will it help children succeed in their careers?

Community Connection

What resources does your community have for finding out about jobs? Use the telephone book and the Internet to make a list. Include resources such as the state employment agency or department of labor, the U.S. Department of Labor and its Web sites, placement offices at schools, and other resources. Visit the Web sites of these organizations and find out the resources that are available.

Review

EXERCISE 13 Answer the Questions

Write the answers in your notebook.

> **The *Occupational Outlook Handbook***
>
> The *Occupational Outlook Handbook* is one of the best resources for finding out about jobs. This huge book is well over 1,000 pages long and covers almost all the jobs available in the U.S. The handbook contains a detailed description of each job plus a lot of additional information, including the education and training required, the pay, and the number of jobs that will become available over the next few years. The *Occupational Outlook Handbook* is published by the U.S. Department of Labor, and you can find copies of it at many libraries or by going online to the department's Web site.

1. What is the *Occupational Outlook Handbook?*
2. Can you find out information about pay?
3. Can you find out information about specific companies?
4. Can you find out information about the education you need to get a certain job?
5. Where can you read the *Occupational Outlook Handbook?*

Your Portfolio

Review the card you wrote in Taking Action on page 120. Put a copy of the sentences in your portfolio.

Summing Up

I can:

- [ ] **1.** Read about jobs that are growing in number.
- [ ] **2.** Read about teaching children about work.
- [ ] **3.** Understand cause-effect relationships.
- [ ] **4.** Understand the future tense with will.
- [ ] **5.** Use a chart to organize information.
- [ ] **6.** ______________________________

Teamwork

For each Teamwork activity, follow the instructions on the unit page or on this page.

Unit 1, Page 5

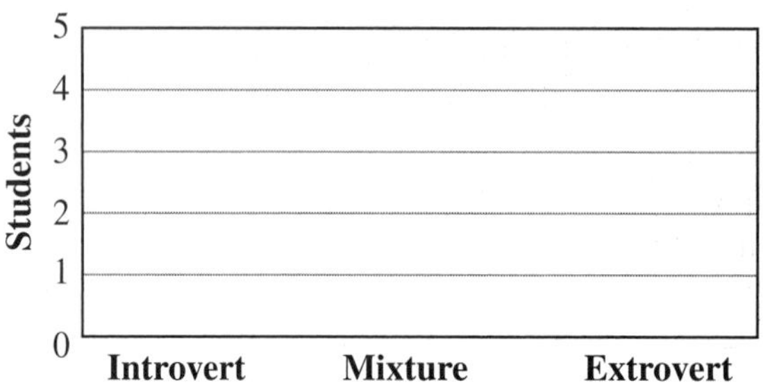

Unit 2, Page 17

Reasons people visit the Mall of America

See a movie or a show	**36%**
Eat	**53%**

Reasons people visit the Mall of America	
Shop	%
Visit the amusement park	%

Unit 3, Page 29

A. Complete the table on page 123. Ask, "What do people in (Mexico) do for good luck at a wedding?" Answer your partner's questions.

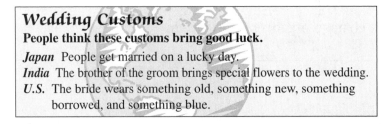

Wedding Customs

People think these customs bring good luck.

Japan People get married on a lucky day.
India The brother of the groom brings special flowers to the wedding.
U.S. The bride wears something old, something new, something borrowed, and something blue.

Country	Good Luck Custom
Mexico	
China	
Morocco	

B. Switch roles and repeat the activity.

Unit 4, Page 41

You want to open a bank account. Read the situations and tell your partner about your needs.

1. You want only a checking account. You can keep about $300 in it.
2. You want a checking account and a savings account. You can keep $1,700 in your accounts. You want interest on your checking account.
3. You want a savings account. You can put about $600 in it right now.

Unit 5, Page 53

Ask your partner questions and complete the chart. Use the information in the table to answer your partner's questions. Then switch roles and repeat the activity.

Caffeine Content

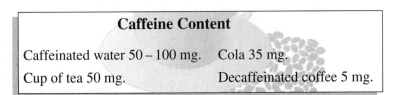

Caffeinated water 50 – 100 mg.	Cola 35 mg.
Cup of tea 50 mg.	Decaffeinated coffee 5 mg.

Food	Caffeine Content
Coffee yogurt	
Chocolate bar	
Cup of coffee	
Diet cola	

Unit 6, Page 65

Edison's Achievements

Lightbulb 1880

Filmed *The Great Train Robbery* 1903

Achievement	Year
Lightbulb	
Records and Record Players	
Movies	
The Great Train Robbery	

Unit 7, Page 77

B. Work with a partner. Student A asks Student B the questions on page 77. Student B writes the answers here. Student A checks Student B's answers. Then switch roles and repeat part B.

Answers

1. ______________________
2. ______________________
3. ______________________
4. ______________________
5. ______________________
6. ______________________

Unit 8, Page 89

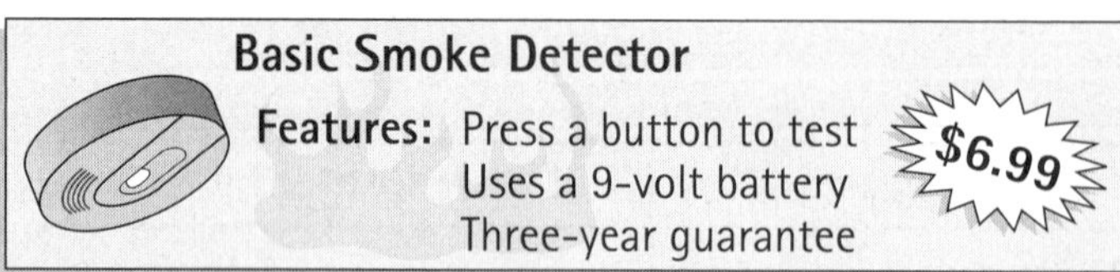

	Premium Smoke Detector	Basic Smoke Detector
How do you test it?		
How much does it cost?		
How long is the guarantee?		

Unit 9, Page 101

Unit 10, Page 113

A. Complete the chart.

Expected Growth in Jobs, 2000-2010	
Medical Assistants	57%
Hotel Desk Clerks	33%
Teacher Assistants	24%

Expected Growth in Jobs, 2000–2010	%
Customer Service Representatives	
Social and Human Service Assistants	
Personal and Home Care Aides	

B. Review your answers to part A and to Exercise 5. Which jobs are growing the fastest? Are you interested in any of the jobs? Why or why not? Tell your ideas to your partner. Share your partner's ideas with the class.

Name: ______________________

Access Reading 3

Date: ______________________

Reading Journal

Class: ______________________

Use this Reading Journal to keep track of your reading. During each unit, make a photocopy of this page and fill it out as you work through the unit. Keep each unit's completed journal in your notebook or portfolio.

Unit _____

Reading 1

Title: ______________________

Main Idea: ______________________

What I learned	What I Want to Learn in the Future

Reading 2

Title: ______________________

Main Idea: ______________________

What I learned	What I Want to Learn in the Future

Additional Readings

I also read these related readings:

What I Read	Main Idea	What I Learned

Vocabulary Index

Skills Index